L2/TR2/BFB

COMBAT REPORT

COMBAT REPORT

THE RAF AND THE FALL OF FRANCE

KATE CAFFREY

The Crowood Press

First published in 1990 by
The Crowood Press
Gipsy Lane, Swindon
Wiltshire SN2 6DQ

British Library Cataloguing in Publication Data
Caffrey, Kate
    Combat report : the RAF and the fall of France.
    1. World War 2. Battle of Britain. Air
    operations by Great Britain, Royal Air Force
    I. Title
    940.5421

        ISBN 1 85223 564 0

Typeset by PCS Typesetting, Frome, Somerset
Printed in Great Britain by Billing & Sons Ltd, Worcester

Contents

. . . He came out under
Nine-tenths cloud, but I was higher.
. . . I let him have a sharp four-second squirt,
Closing to fifty yards. He went on fire.

John Pudney, *Combat Report* (1942)

Sooner or later
Most lonely in all men, pity
Must still be met
Alone, perhaps in tatters at high noon.

John Pudney, *Sooner or Later* (1943)

To those members of the Royal Air Force, living and dead,
who did what is recorded here

Acknowledgements

It has given me much pleasure to have the opportunity of writing this book. I have often wished for the chance of writing about the Royal Air Force. In 1940, at home for the summer holidays from school in the country, the sight of dog-fights in the sky was part of everyday life; the fighter pilots were, rightly, everybody's heroes.

I regret that Bomber Command does not figure more largely in this account. It cannot be helped: in the period covered by this book, Bomber Command had not reached its full power – through no fault of its own. Also, in the demands and conditions of the time, it was Fighter Command which had to take the central role. Bomber Command came into its own in the following year and won its great honours from then on: as 'Bomber' Harris himself said in his farewell speech to his Command in 1946: If any one asks you what you did in the War, you are perfectly entitled to say "I won it".'

Those who are interested in the history of the War should make a point of seeing good films made at the time or near enough. There is more to a film than the story, or the actors, or the photography: there is the atmosphere. Films with important factual backgrounds made by people who were not alive at the time often miss this, and can go wrong on tiny details (the WAAF hair-styles in The Battle of Britain, for example). It makes one wonder how accurate a historical portrayal can ever be. A selection of admirable films that got it right – and there were many – would have to include, taking the War as a whole, the following baker's dozen: A Canterbury Tale, The Dam Busters, Dunkirk, Fires Were Started, The First of the Few, The Gentle Sex, In Which We Serve, Millions Like Us, One of our Aircraft is Missing, The Way to the Stars, Western Approaches, and, two examples from the opposite camp, Triumph of the Will, and Sieg im Westen. People who clearly remember the war will doubtless have their own choices to add to this list.

Someone is certain to notice that this book contains no mention of 'the question of the twenty-five squadrons', a heatedly argued controversy which takes up pages in many accounts. Churchill gave that figure as Dowding's estimate of the basic requirement. Dowding gave it as fifty-two. My own opinion may sound frivolous, but is quite as likely as any other: that whoever supplied Churchill with that figure simply made the very common slip of scribbling the number down back to front.

I am grateful to many people for their help with this book. First on the list must come the Staff of the splendid Royal Air Force Museum at Hendon, especially Mr Peter Murton for allowing me access to the excellent Archives and permitting me to include brief quotations from the volumes of Combat Reports to be found there. All the Museum Staff readily answered questions and took pains to point out special exhibits, like the Blue Spitfire and the recently acquired Messerschmidt 109.

I am grateful to the Officer Commanding and to the President of the Mess Committee at Bentley Priory for letting me visit it, and to Squadron Leader Brian Canfer for showing me round that historic place.

I thank the publishing house of Cassell very much for giving permission to quote the extract from Churchill's speech in the House of Commons on 4 June 1940, a speech printed in Volume Two of Sir Winston's *The Second World War* (a work which I possess in the Reprint Society eighth edition of 1955).

Those members of the Royal Air Force who wrote and talked to me, saying generously: ' Make what use you like of this', earned my deep gratitude. They include: Air Chief Marshal Sir Harry Broadhurst, KCB, CB, KBE, DSO*, DFC*, AFC; Air Chief Marshall Sir Christopher Foxley-Norris, GCB, DSO, OBE, MA; Wing Commander I. G. Cosby, DFC, who joined the Royal Air Force in 1938 and who in 1940 was based at Douai with Lysander Squadron 13 before getting away from Cherbourg after France fell, when he was stationed at Hooton Park in the Wirral, occupied with anti-invasion exercises; Wing Commander Peter Parrott, AFC, DFC*; Group Captain Denis David, CBE, AFC, DFC*.

I also thank Clive I. Fleay, Esq., for his assistance, advice and interest, and, of course, my publishers, particularly Antony Bird, Esq., who commissioned the work and who proved a model of his profession.

Kate Caffrey
London 1990

1

Rules of the Game

Yours is the instrument, the traffic of air.
Its magic has caught you, and gifted you and your like,
Caparisoned you with the power to swoop and strike.

John Pudney

We have all seen him. Films have made us agreeably familiar with the image of the pilot, somehow closely observed by us through his windscreen (which, as the old mathematical conclusion beloved of generations of pupils says, is impossible). But what is he actually doing, and how did he get there?

A young man accepted by the Royal Air Force for pilot training before the War was taught his profession in a less high-pressured atmosphere than it was for those who came later, when the need was urgent. This is not to say that the wartime training was less thorough, but there was less time to practise, so it had to be more intensive. To balance this was the new awareness, the new urgency, so that, while the later recruits were light-hearted still, they knew that as soon as they were qualified they must be prepared to meet the real thing, even on reconnaissance or convoy duty. For in wartime a fight is always round the next corner.

The first thing any aspiring pilot had to have was what was called air experience. This was not only the experience of flight. Just as all sailors must learn what the sea is like in all its moods, and all soldiers are well advised to learn how to read a landscape, so airmen will profit by lying flat on the ground and studying the sky – the movements of cloud and wind, the flight of birds. Clouds are of great importance, as they contain turbulence, and in the biggest clouds, the giant thunderheads reaching up to forty thousand feet, aircraft can be broken to pieces. A man in training would fly first as a passenger, in a two-seater plane with the instructor behind him: the little Tiger Moths were often used for this at first. There would be two sets of controls so that, if the learner made a mistake when in control, the instructor could take over, as he could if the pupil looked like ditching them both.

Handling the controls and learning what they would do was the next step. Then came taxiing, driving the aircraft like a motor along the ground. Following this was a string of skills: straight and level flying, climbing, gliding, medium turns with and without the engine. Stalling was closely examined. Next was the take-off, including the important take-off into the wind (not advisable for Tiger Moths), approaches and

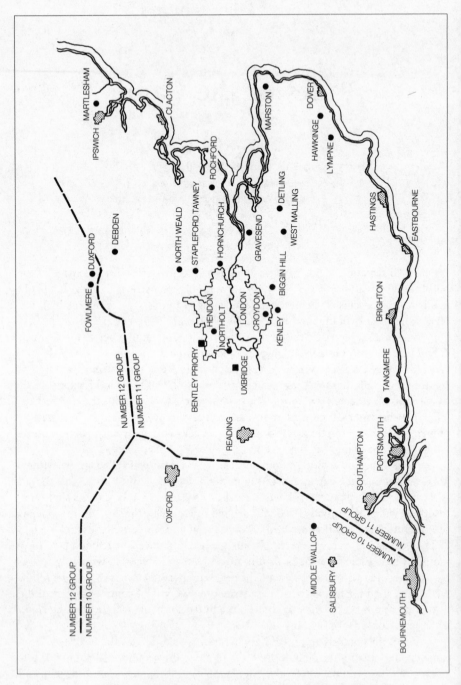

Fighter Command Airfields in South-eastern England, 1940.

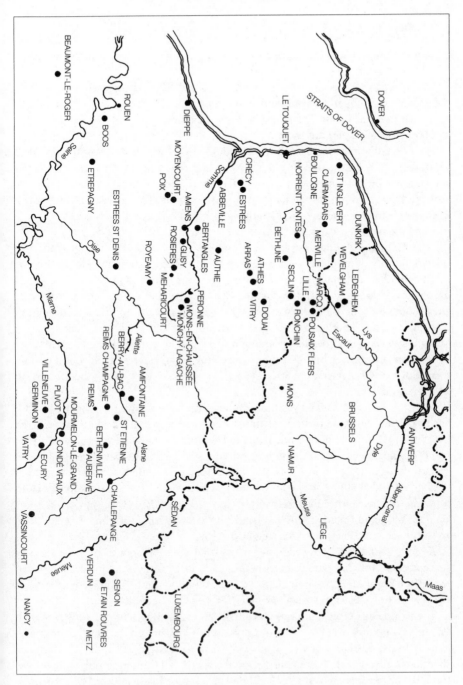

Airfields used in France and Belgium by the RAF, September 1939–June 1940

landings. The wind-sock on every airfield was helpful up to a point. If it hung limp, there was nothing to worry about, there could be no wind as near as made no difference. But if it stood straight out from its mast, there was no telling whether the wind was a good breeze or a full gale.

One special skill was described in the manuals as preliminary action in case of fire. There was stopping and starting the engine in flight, whether in case of fire or not, and what to do in a spin. The first solo flight, a big moment, had to be made within ten hours' flying time, not more.

Further accomplishments followed: sideslipping, which was apparently most enjoyable, more instruction in case of fire, which was after all the airman's greatest menace, low-level flying which was never done without the instructor until the pupil was proficient, steep turns with and without the engine. There were climbing turns. There were forced landings, and landings with and without the engine.

Instrument flying was a weird experience, pulling a green canvas hood over the cockpit and flying 'blind', hoping all the time that the instructor was watching like a hawk for any other planes near by. Pupils had to practise stopping and starting the engine in the air, taking-off and landing in cross-winds, and what were called aerobatics – loops and rolls, for example, which were not just for show, or for fun, they could save your life. There was air navigation to learn, and tests for forced landings and cross-country flights. Pupils soon learnt to look out for helpful landmarks. A straight stretch of river or canal pointing in the right direction was the best, far easier to see than any railway, but there were church towers and spires, roads running along a crest of bare hill, even a small lake, which were useful for guiding them home, at any rate in daylight.

Alongside all that was the ground training. This started with the theory of flight, incorporating the three theories of thrust, drag and lift. Scientist-pilots, among the greatest of whom had been Lindemann and Tizard, had taught everyone how to get out of a spin: the natural impulse is to pull the stick back, but that only tightens the spin, so what must be done is to push the stick forward and push the opposite rudder. And hope, added H.R. Allen, who was nicknamed 'Dizzy' after an occasion in 1940 when he put his Spitfire into an inverted spin, the most dangerous spin of all. Pilots on training might find their engines labouring and controls heavy on practice climbs to thirty thousand feet, at which height they had to inhale oxygen.

As they ended their early training, pilots tried their best not to be passed out as 'exceptional', for that would mean being made instructors in their turn. They had joined the Royal Air Force to fight, not to teach others to fight. The great number who truly were exceptional revealed it when they were on operations.

Then came advanced training. One flight at a time was sent out for Armament Practice. They shot at big squares of canvas set up on the ground, and at drogues – akin to a kind of flight-buoy or wind-sock – towed at a hundred miles an hour: not the most realistic of exercises considering the speed of a Messerschmidt (three times that), but all practice was something.. The airfield Duty Pilot, firing a red Véry cartridge to warn other aircraft to stay clear, ordered take-off for the battle climb, the full-throttle ascent to over thirty thousand feet, with plenty of reminders about oxygen. Some pilots

Fighter Command. A fighter pilot of the RAF, 30 June 1940.

on training were told to fire into the sea. They found, doing this, that the recoil of their guns could cut the rate of climb by as much as forty miles an hour.

There were practice dog-fights. A dog-fight, which became a familiar sight in southern England in the summer of 1940, was a duel between two fighter planes. The sight of the big oval vapour-trails from the two tiny shapes in the sky is one that

5

thousands of people can still remember. Pilots experienced the ear-blocking known to everyone climbing rapidly to a high altitude, or for that matter travelling on high-speed trains through tunnels or in fast cars on mountain roads. The cure apparently was to pinch the nose and puff down it. In the early stages a dog-fight was a more hit or miss business than it later became. The advantage went to the pilot who dived with the sun behind him and could therefore surprise the other.

The practice dog-fights taught many lessons, but were not to be compared with the real thing, where the Germans' greater experience showed techniques which were adopted and included in training. One valuable lesson was to fly loose, as the Germans did, not in close formation 'like an air display', as seasoned pilots disparagingly put it. One advantage the Luftwaffe had was that their aircraft, fuelled by direct injection, could dive untroubled, but the Royal Air Force planes had carburettors which would flood and stall the engine for a moment. Also the Luftwaffe camouflage paint was better. But their aircraft had higher wing-loading, so the Spitfires and Hurricanes were more manoeuvrable.

Before the War, it was a Royal Air Force saying that 'only fools and owls fly at night'. Now this had all changed. Now the pilots' final advanced tests were night take-offs and landings along with the dog-fight exercises. Those who met the requirements were 'passed operational', and as a rule the first duties given to them were to protect small coastal convoys. This had hazards that an outsider would never have thought of. Neither the Royal Navy nor the Merchant Navy seemed to know much, if anything, about aircraft recognition and, on the simple basis that ships cost more than planes and therefore must take every precaution, were apt to fire on any aircraft they saw. There were compensations, though. One patrol that gave a pilot a truly breathtaking sight was on escort of HMS *Ajax*, coming home for repairs after the Battle of the River Plate.

All pilots soon learnt to have the deepest respect for their fitters. These men had passed through the most thorough of courses which included the theory and practice of aircraft engineering as well as a wide variety of drills, and knowledge of Royal Air Force Law for good measure. It was not just that they were absolutely reliable: they were wonderfully ingenious with the machines they loved, ready to die for them if need be, and a good number of them did. Their discipline was excellent. The speed with which they soon learnt to re-fuel and re-arm any aircraft suggests the amazing and super-efficient pit-stop work in a Grand Prix motor race. And after every flight they wanted, and insisted on getting, minutely detailed reports of the smallest fault, and their investigation of each one could not have been more meticulous.

It was a considerable job making, and keeping, aircraft serviceable, especially in periods of much action. Usually each aircraft had two men working on it, the fitter and the rigger. The fitter was the mechanic responsible for the engine. The rigger attended to the wiring, the control column and the controls generally. Each aircraft had to have the correct amount of fuel – not only petrol, but the coolant glycol to cool the engine, and the proper oil. Radiators and petrol-pipes were checked for the slightest trace of a leak. Bullet-holes had to be patched and repaired. Engines had to be gone over with the most finicking care. The guns were serviced by the armourers, who re-armed and checked them after every action.

The green 100-octane petrol was supplied from tanks called bowsers which could hold more than eight hundred gallons. The bowser-driver wore a boiler-suit and gumboots. His job had one unique disadvantage, as he reeked of petrol more or less all the time, despite thorough washing, and as he walked about the airfield he presented a curiously spectral appearance, as he was surrounded by a yellow aura of petrol fumes.

If these mechanics and technicians were excellent, so were the Non-Commissioned Officers, who, as in all the Services at all times, formed the backbone of every unit. They were almost invariably calm, solid as rocks, and they stood no nonsense. The Royal Air Force NCOs had been trained in the best school anywhere, the Royal Air Force Technical School at Halton near Winchester. Without them, and without the ground mechanics, the Royal Air Force could have done nothing, and every man who flew knew it.

One feature of Royal Air Force life that infuriated everyone regardless of rank or duties was the job of moving from one airfield to another, as it usually meant that a squadron would be out of action for at least forty-eight hours. Every move began with the Advance Party, NCOs and ground crews with their tools and heavy equipment like cranes and jacks, along with enough kit to provide accommodation for all concerned, and their motor transport. These would set out by road for the new base. All aircraft were made ready for take-off and would then wait for the order, timed so that they would arrive when the Advance Party had had long enough to be ready to receive them. They spent much of the waiting-time hoping fervently that nothing had happened to hold up the Advance Party, either en route or on arrival. Once the aircraft had flown off, the Rear Party would clear up, complete the inventory of every piece of equipment accounted for, leave the airfield and its buildings as tidy as possible, and then follow, either in trucks or by train.

It is interesting to compare the British training with that of the Germans.

The first obvious difference is the matter of names: the Luftwaffe were considered as part of the Army, so all Luftwaffe personnel had Army rank. Heinz Knoke, a German fighter pilot who wrote an account of his career (I flew for the Führer, 1953) volunteered in the early summer of 1939 when he was eighteen, looking for a military career combined with what he called the beauty and freedom of the air. In this respect he, like many of his fellows, closely resembled his British opposite numbers. He went on to score fifty-two enemy aircraft shot down. The preliminary examination, the most thorough, wide-ranging and exacting of his life, lasted four days. The first day was taken up with immensely precise medical checks. The second put the candidates through written essays, impromptu talks, and answering questions from officers and psychiatrists. On the third day the candidates were spun in rotating chairs and made to crawl through low-pressure chambers, immediately after which they had to assemble sets of small gears and cog-wheels, a timed process designed to test their reactions to lack of oxygen. The fourth day had a strenuous athletic programme: running (long-distance and sprint), jumping, discus and javelin, also boxing,

7

swimming and gymnastics. Knoke and his fellow recruits then went home to wait for the verdict. It was late July.

They were all startled in late August by newspaper reports of 'Polish atrocities against the German minority in Poland'. That this was a piece of skilful stage-management by the German government never occurred to them. They accepted it as a fact, and it made the subsequent invasion of Poland seem perfectly logical and reasonable. But they were astonished by the French and British declaration of war. It seemed ages to wait for their call-up, but at last, in November, it came. Their basic training was not unlike the British system, except for a few odd details: on the first solo flight, for example, red streamers flew from the learner's wing-tips to warn others to keep clear ('if you value your life' the learners would add to one another). And their Pilot's Certificate was a flamboyant affair, appointing each young man 'in the name of the Führer' to the rank of Lieutenant, and adding:

I confirm this appointment in full expectation that through conscientious perform-ance of his duty as an officer in accordance with his oath of service and loyalty, confidence shown to the above-named will be justified. He on his part may call upon the special protection of the Führer.

It was signed by Goering and presented with the ceremonial dagger of an officer.

One item of clothing in the Royal Air Force had a pedigree going right back to the Royal Flying Corps: the forage cap. Practical as well as historic, it could be folded into a pocket. Flying overalls lined with rubber, leather jackets lined with wool, and pure silk parachutes were supplied by the Irving Company. The jackets were too bulky to squeeze into the narrow cockpit of a Spitfire, but were all right in a Hurricane, and had the advantage of giving protection against flying bits of metal. The parachutes used so much silk that one pilot had three pairs of lovely silk pyjamas made out of a half-destroyed one. (Later the parachutes were of man-made fibres.) It was important to adjust the parachute-straps precisely, neither too tight nor too loose, and each one had to be dried out and inspected at least once a month. Invaluable against the cold – temperatures could be minus fifty at thirty thousand feet – were the leather gauntlets with their silk inner gloves, the thick woollen knee-socks and wool-lined suede boots. These boots, and more and more flying-jackets as time went on, were made by Morland's of Glastonbury. Finally there was the leather flying-helmet, with its oxygen-mask fastened to one side and press-stud clip on the other, and radio-earphones in the ear-pieces, their wires connected to the microphone in the mask. (German pilots had throat-microphones transmitting from the vocal cords, which were rather better.) The Irving Company started the Caterpillar Club: a pilot who baled-out to save his life was sent a tiny gold caterpillar brooch. If the plane had been on fire at the time the caterpillar had jewelled red eyes, otherwise the eyes were jewelled green.

Let us take a look at what the Spitfire pilot saw when he eased himself into his seat in the cockpit.

On his right was a large black lever. He had to pump this back and forth, anything up to thirty times, to get the undercarriage to retract. As the wheels tucked inside their cells he would hear a thump, whereupon the canvas covers slid over the wheel-cells.

Above this lever were five gauges: oil pressure, fuel availability; engine boost, radiator temperature, and the engine rev counter. The centre of the instrument panel held the indicators for turn and slip and for the rate of climb and descent, the artificial horizon and the gyro-compass, the Air Speed Indicator and the altimeter. This was always adjusted on the ground according to the air-pressure figures supplied by the weather-men.

Above, close to the wind-shield, was the gun-sight, and below it was the compass. On the left were the flying position indicator and the flap control. The gadget that always comes to mind first, in the early days charmingly named the joystick, was now simply the stick. It was in the centre, closer to the pilot.

The Spitfire Mark I's handle on the engine-throttle was made of bone, which was somehow more interesting and attractive than the wooden one in the Mark II.

'Dizzy' Allen has described his first flight in a Spitfire. One young man has likened the moment when the aircraft is given full power and starts to hurtle along the runway for take-off to the run-up of a first class fast bowler in a Test Match, a good comparison. Allen started his run, giving the throttle full boost, which was 1,030 horse-power, and eased the stick back. He selected the 'undercarriage up' and pumped the black lever vigorously. The earliest Spitfires had a tendency to nose up and down when this was done, so Supermarine soon added weights inside the elevator controls to correct it. When the thump told him that the wheels had retracted, his green lights turned red, so he knew that the undercarriage was firmly up and locked into place.

It took him thirteen minutes from take-off to reach the height of the battle-climb, 30,000 feet, compared with the Hurricane's seventeen minutes. Having put his oxygen on to emergency flow in good time, he could now ease it back.

He then began to put the Spitfire through its paces. He tested the switch-off of the magnetos in turn, then the trim of the rudder, then the elevator bias. The aircraft was wonderfully sensitive: it only needed tiny adjustments to fly straight and level. He flew for a moment with his hands off the controls. Then he practised rolls and loops.

Returning to the airfield, he came into the proper circuit anti-clockwise, put the undercarriage down when he was correctly down wind, and turned in for the final approach. He lowered the flaps and touched down, as he had hoped to do, on three points, the wheels and the tail-skid touching simultaneously. There was a slight bump upwards, then all the wheels were moving forward on the grass. The long nose of the Spitfire tilted up when it was grounded, blocking the view, so he had to put his head out to make sure he was going straight. When the speed had slowed enough not to tip the aircraft forward at the stop, he gently applied the brakes. Keeping them on, he used enough power to steer across to the perimeter, and taxied back, moving the Spitfire's nose from left to right to make sure there was no obstruction in the way. He parked in a line of aircraft near the flight huts and switched off the engine.

The Hurricane was not as fast as the Spitfire and, partly owing to films made at the time, like the 1942 film *The First of the Few*, had less glamour to the public. It was quicker to notice and resent a pilot's mistakes if he did not handle it right, and in its early days there were some fatal accidents. But those who flew it soon learnt its qualities and then they swore by it. It was particularly popular with the ground staff, as it was easier than the Spitfire to service and repair. It was tough and well-built, absolutely solid during action with its eight Browning machine-guns, and highly manoeuvrable. It provided an excellent view despite, or because of, its bigger cockpit. Its Merlin engines were nothing short of magnificent. One pilot who expressed his admiration and love for the Hurricane was Peter Townsend, another was Michael Maxwell. All fighter pilots noticed the characteristic smell as they took their seats in either fighter: a mixture of engine oil and 100-octane petrol plus the special coating painted on the canvas over the gun-ports. But they spoke of both aircraft in lyrical terms. The Spitfire was superb – so well-balanced it would fly itself – if a pilot passed out for lack of oxygen the Spitfire would go into a dive which would bring him round. One pilot said it had an excellent effect on his character, making him nearly as well-balanced as itself. The Hurricane was a dream aeroplane – absolutely super – marvellously springy undercarriage, beautiful softness of feel. It gave confidence, its engine was so good, its guns so powerful, its structure so tough, so well built for war. It flew strongly and fast. It was wonderfully manoeuvrable. The Spitfire was more agile, and it won on looks: it looked right, which meant it *was* right. But both were marvellous and each had its devotees. Townsend called the Hurricane 'a thoroughbred'. Allen said the Spitfire was 'perfection'.

Curiously enough, the Luftwaffe developed what has been called 'Spitfire snobbery'. A Luftwaffe pilot preferred to say he had been shot down by a Spitfire, whether this were true or not, because it seemed to give him more prestige. Comparatively few Spitfires were in the Battle of France, yet according to Luftwaffe claims there were dozens. The Hurricane outnumbered the Spitfire in a ratio of about three to two throughout 1940. Machine for machine, throughout the Battle of Britain, both did equally well, the Hurricane having a slight edge. But both, rightly, became a legend, and they still are.

In the Royal Air Force units sent to France there were four Lysander squadrons: 2, 4, 13 and 26 Squadrons. Christopher Foxley-Norris who flew in them, later to become an Air Chief Marshal, when asked about the Lysander, said simply: 'It was a very good aircraft for the Great War.' In other words, good for reconnaissance and observation, and indeed it was used for these purposes back in England. 'In France we lost the lot, we came out on foot – what was left of us'. The history of the Lysander in May and June 1940 is a tragic one.

Many men came into the Royal Air Force by way of the university air squadrons. These were very popular before the War among those undergraduates who were attracted by flying. Some joined them for other reasons as well. To be able to appear in public wearing an officer's uniform was a great help in meeting attractive girls. At that time, of course, boys and girls in public and grammar schools were almost all in separate establishments, and on going up to the university one of the amenities that made eyes sparkle was the prospect of meeting dozens of the opposite sex. Apart from that, the university air squadrons gave future pilots and air crews a very good start.

On the other hand, one must never underestimate the Flight Sergeants: they made up about a third of the fighter crews and must therefore have at least a third of the credit.

Michael Maxwell's background has some unusual features. His eldest brother, Gerald, twenty-two when Michael was born, had been a distinguished pilot with the Royal Flying Corps in the Great War. Michael Maxwell expected an Army career: at Ampleforth School he was a corporal in the OTC and in 1935, aged eighteen, received his Lieutenant's commission in the Queen's Own Cameron Highlanders. Going up to Oxford in 1936 he joined the Oxford University Air Squadron and was thus able to go to camp each year with both Army and Air personnel. In the spring of 1939 he applied for a permanent commission in the Royal Air Force and was accepted on 28 August. He therefore had to resign from the Army, and, while waiting for this to be completed, served as a soldier. On 10 October he was told to report at the Flying Training School at Hullavington in Wiltshire, where the entire intake was composed of people like himself with university air squadron backgrounds, and were given the best instructors anywhere, in his opinion. His elder brother had served in 56 Squadron, and he joined that Squadron at its base at North Weald on 20 April 1940. He was convinced it was the finest of all squadrons when he watched twelve Hurricanes take off in formation with what he called stunningly flawless style. Walking down to the

Air Marshal Sir Keith Park at the cockpit of a Harvard aircraft.

hangars the first morning, he met an obviously very senior officer indeed, who asked where the Commanding Officer was, where his office was, and, when Maxwell said he had no idea, how long he had been there. To Maxwell's reply that he was on his way there, the visitor laughed and said: 'Come with me and we'll find them together'. He was Air Vice-Marshal Sir Keith Park.

Harry Broadhurst joined the Royal Air Force in 1926 at the age of twenty-one, and, like Maxwell, he preferred fighters to bombers. Between 1933 and 1936 he was Officer Commanding 111 Squadron and in 1937 was awarded the Air Force Cross. He was unexpectedly shifted in 1938 to Northolt to command 111 Squadron again: the former Commander had blotted his copy-book, having gone absent without leave in pursuit of a beautiful and much admired actress who, presumably wishing to discourage her suitor, hit him over the head with a champagne bottle in the most fashionable night club of the day, whereupon the story came out and the unfortunate officer was court-martialled, so Broadhurst took over. When the War started he was Squadron Leader of Hurricane 1 Squadron; the most prestigious, but, according to him, he had not yet learnt when not to make cheerful suggestions to those in high places. The Luftwaffe at that time took to bombing shipping in the Firth of Forth and Broadhurst, meeting Sir Hugh Dowding himself in the Mess one day, remarked: 'Why don't you send a decent squadron up there to deal with them, sir?' Dowding's expression did not change, and he said nothing, but next day 1 Squadron was posted to Scotland.

In January 1940 Broadhurst was on Squadron Leader Training when Sir Keith Park appointed him Acting Wing Commander. At the beginning of May he was sent to command Coltishall, a brand-new peace-time designed Fighter Station:

> When I arrived there were no aircraft on the Station – only admin staff and engineers preparing it for the arrival of three fighter squadrons.

What he did later will be told in its due place, but at Coltishall he had his initials, H B, painted on his Hurricane – which he too thought the world of.

Two of the most famous fighter pilots are Tom Gleave and Geoffrey Page. They do not come directly into this account but they must be mentioned for their background. Gleave was undeniably elderly as pilots go, thirty years old in 1938. As a child at Walton, Liverpool, he fell in love with flying when his uncle was appointed Aircraft Disposal Officer at Aintree airfield and invited the boy to visit it. One world-famous airman he saw there was Alan Cobham, a Great War ace who went on to pioneer long-distance flights and to win among other trophies the King's Cup and the Britannia Trophy. Gleave became a fighter pilot in the Thirties and was actually on leave when the war broke out. On 2 May 1940 he was in charge of 253 Squadron, which during the Battle of France suffered considerable losses so that by the middle of June it consisted of a few very young 'veterans' and equally young inexperienced men. Gleave, impatiently fretting for action, had to stay at the base, too old and, after promotion to Wing Commander in July, too senior to lead his squadron in battle according to those older and more senior still, but he asked the Group Thirteen Commander-in-Chief, Air Vice-Marshal Richard 'Birdie' Saul, if he could drop his rank and be put on operations. The newly appointed Squadron Leader Starr was sympathetic and generously suggested that he and Gleave might 'share' the squadron between them. Gleave joyfully went back on operations and did spectacularly well until the last day of August when both he and Starr were shot down, Starr being killed and Gleave receiving dreadful injuries which put him in the hands of Fighter Command's hero surgeon, Archibald McIndoe. When his wife first set eyes on him she was outwardly composed and brave enough merely to ask what on earth he had been doing. Gleave's answer became the title of his 1941 book: 'Had a row with a German.'

Page, twenty years old in 1940, had trained at Cranwell and by August was a 'veteran'. His courage and daring impressed everyone but, according to him, he always had to struggle against fear. (Of course this is true of the very bravest people.) He felt that the air-fights were too often 'butchery'. He was shot down on 12 August with terrible burns and he too was expertly treated by Mr McIndoe (later Sir Archibald). He had many major operations – some say fifteen, some say seventeen – and he vowed to shoot down that number of the enemy to pay for it. He did so. At least one Air Chief Marshal has said: 'He certainly qualifies for the VC'.

Richard George Arthur Barclay, always called George, son of a vicar, was not quite twenty when the War started. He was educated at Stowe and Trinity College, Cambridge, where he joined the University Air Squadron in October 1938. They did their flying at Duxford where life was very pleasant, spare-time pursuits including shooting and hunting. During the Long Vacation of 1939 eighty of the Squadron spent those summer weeks on full-time training at Duxford, where Barclay totalled ninety-three flying hours in the Avro Tutor aircraft they used.

He qualified as a Pilot Officer in October and on 8 November reported to Number Three Initial Training Wing, based at Hastings in that splendid piece of Thirties building dominating the west end of the front, Marine Court. One Physical Training Sergeant there was the celebrated boxer Len Harvey and one of the Pilot Officer Instructors was the former Test cricketer Walter Hammond. Barclay passed out at Christmas and, after Christmas leave, went to Cranwell as one of thirty-five pilots for war training, the first such course held there. Its calibre was described tersely as 'above average'. Barclay went on to Cranwell's Advanced Training Squadron and did well. He spent a week in early June flying Lysanders at the Number One School of Army Co-operation at Old Sarum and then joined the Officers' Training Unit at Aston Down in Gloucestershire. One eminent pilot who preceded him there had been Richard Hillary, ex-University Air Squadron, Oxford, who in his time at Aston Down had caused a sensation by flying his Spitfire under one of the Severn bridges: Barclay repeated the feat. He spent some time on formation flying practice, a technique already outmoded by the Luftwaffe's methods. The course ended on 23 June when Barclay was posted to the five-week-old 249 Squadron at Leconfield in Yorkshire, where he flew Hurricanes. The Squadron Leader was Richard Kellett, famous later as Commanding Officer of the Polish 303 Squadron. In the third week of July 'Birdie' Saul sent them a congratulatory letter on having done more than a thousand flying hours in a month, something never achieved before as far as he knew, which, he rightly remarked, reflected the greatest credit on all concerned.

Apart from uneventful patrols, Barclay did not get into action until mid-August, after which he had combats in plenty. Not quite two years later Acting Squadron Leader George Barclay, DFC, was shot down and killed in North Africa.

'The pre-war Royal Air Force was a club,' says Denis David, who was then a Pilot Officer and whose first wartime flight was on 8 September 1939 from Debden to Vitry-en-Artois near Arras. He was well aware, even then, of the carefully built chain of command and operation and what it leads to, ending 'with the boy who fires the gun, he's the one who wins the war for you'. We shall meet Mr David again later.

Peter Parrott, a Pilot Officer who had just completed a course on Hurricanes at Group Eleven's Fighter Pool, reported to 607 Squadron on 23 January 1940. At that time 607 and 615 Squadrons made up Number Sixty Wing of the Air Component assigned to the British Expeditionary Force in France. It was based at Vitry-en-Artois and the aircraft were Gladiator biplanes. Number Sixty-one Wing, based near Lille, consisted of (Hurricane) 85 and 87 Squadrons. These four squadrons, says Parrott,

> were the total fighter force supporting the BEF at the time.
>
> In April we started to re-equip with Hurricanes. I was the only member of the Squadron who had flown a Hurricane, and so had the privilege of ferrying the first one from Glisy near Rouen to Vitry on 6 April. By 10 May the whole Squadron had converted to the new aircraft. 615 Squadron started to re-equip a week or two after us and were still training up.
>
> Before 10 May our only operational flying had been occasional patrols over Northern France along the Belgian border, and giving cover to cross-Channel shipping, all in the Gladiators. Since there was no Radar and no radio control it was not surprising that the only hostile aircraft we had seen was the occasional very high-flying reconnaissance aircraft, which the Gladiators had no possible chance of intercepting.

One fact that emerges with blinding clarity from all accounts made by, or about, all who flew aircraft in war is that the main, often the only, reason why they chose that Service was the flying itself. It charmed, exhilarated and fascinated them. This applies whether they were in fighters or bombers. Many people, realising that the two kinds require different skills, have asked what makes a good fighter pilot or a good bomber pilot: are there two clear-cut different types of man? Pilots themselves say no, it is not a question of type or temperament, the job makes the man. A possible guide to choice might, however, be that the fighter pilot enjoys the solitary control of his own machine while the bomber pilot is part of a crew and, whether he welcomes this or not, he feels responsible for them. But just looking at the photographs of pilots in groups, taken without aircraft in the background, it is not possible as a rule to state with certainty which are which. One set of grinning young men looks very like another, and this goes for both sides. The only safe thing to say is that they joined an air force because they loved the whole concept of flight.

One point that should be made right away is that the men who are doing the actual fighting, in whatever Service, do not as a rule have any idea of what is going on in

14

a battle as a whole, let alone in a war as a whole. This holds true in all wars. At the end of each day each man knows what his particular unit has done and seen, but little or nothing else, except in the vaguest terms. 'X Company was badly shot up', 'There was a lot going on somewhere to the north of us', 'HMS Y was firing all her guns when I last saw her', 'Another squadron joined in' is usually as much as the inquirer will get from any individual who has been in the middle of the fighting. Many who went to France with the Royal Air Force in 1940 simply say: 'We were there getting shot at – what the war as a whole was doing we hadn't a clue'. One former pilot said: 'People ask nowadays, What did you think of Dowding? We didn't know him, or indeed any Commander – if we caught sight of so much as a Group Captain we hid behind a hut'. Of course, and this too must be borne in mind, fighting men of all ranks are given to understatement.

The most famous command in 1940 was the one-word order 'scramble'. Fighter pilots knew whether they were to be in a state of readiness and at what notice – immediate, thirty minutes, or whatever – and those on immediate readiness were on their airfield, on the grass or in a nearby hut. Their aircraft were waiting, pointed the same way, fuelled-up and serviced. As most fighter airfields had no runways, the planes were positioned on the grass. Some pilots preferred to put their parachutes, helmets and gloves in the plane, others held on to them: it was a matter of individual taste.

'Scramble!' RAF pilots running towards their aircraft, 25 July 1940.

In the months of May, June, and July daylight came early, so the first pilots were out at dawn. The invaluable Navy, Army and Air Force (NAAFI) supply-vans brought refreshments out to them: sometimes bacon and egg breakfasts (often a bit tepid or congealing), more often sandwiches and flasks of tea or coffee. Ground crews, who had frequently worked during the night to repair damaged aircraft, and whose armourers had put in the ammunition of every gun, had completed their meticulous checks and started work on the next flights. On the order 'scramble' each pilot grabbed up his belongings, ran to his aircraft, jumped in, pressed the starter and set off. The number of sorties a day varied according to what was happening. During periods of great pressure, like the Battle of Britain, fighter pilots made several sorties a day one after another, landing only long enough for re-fuelling and re-arming. From the start of training each pilot had his log-book, a stiff-backed volume with each double page ruled in columns headed with the date, type and designation of aircraft, crew, action and time taken. The times were totalled at the foot of the page and carried forward so that the record of flying-hours was there for all to see. An example of this is taken from the log-book of a very famous pilot indeed, Douglas Bader, who recorded two rather interesting sorties dated July 1940, one on the 11th and one on the 13th. Both were in Hurricane D (D being the designation), both list the crew as 'self'. The first sortie, timed at thirty minutes, noted 'Attacked and destroyed one Dornier 17 off Cromer (confirmed)'. The other, timed at one hour and eighteen minutes, reads: 'Attempted interception of Heinkel. Never saw it.'

Reactions to being in readiness waiting for the order to scramble varied considerably. More often than not it was the youngest pilots, the less experienced, who were less profoundly affected, though even they felt keyed-up while waiting. Those who had weathered a number of actions often carried something away from these waiting-periods that they never quite lost. Christopher Foxley-Norris, now a retired Air Chief Marshal, recollects sitting in the dispersal-hut, perhaps reading, perhaps having a game of cards, and everyone going very still when the telephone rang, all eyes following the orderly as he went to answer it. Quite often the call had nothing to do with a scramble, but the tension was always there. He still dislikes hearing a telephone ring, fifty years after.

On the other hand a former Flight Sergeant who had been thankful to quit his uneventful office job and enter the glamorous Royal Air Force said that the scramble was the most exciting thing in the world. It might be quite a bit nervy, as he put it, while you were sitting in a deck-chair and playing games, but the moment the order rang out it was wonderful – dashing to one's aircraft full tilt, perhaps as much as a hundred yard run, and usually finding one of the fitters sitting in the cockpit. The instant the fitter heard the shout of 'scramble' and saw the green Véry pistol-shot that accompanied it he had started the engine, so he now jumped out, the pilot jumped in, fastened his straps, opened the throttle and was away, if possible all within two minutes, which was everyone's aim. According to this young man, he and his friends were worried stiff after the fall of France, in case the war might be over and they would have to leave all the fun and the thrills and go back to dreary normality. They did not worry long. Churchill's speeches assured them that the War was not going to end yet.

On the subject of Fighter Command orders, it was Dowding who made certain that these were simple and could be readily adapted to circumstances. In addition to the unmistakable 'scramble', there was 'angels', used to mean thousands of feet in height, and, as experience grew and techniques developed, the term could be used to deceive. Great emphasis was placed on flying high enough to be above the enemy when attacking, this made all the difference, but the enemy might be listening, so pilots were given to understand that 'Angels eighteen' really meant 'Angels twenty-one' – three thousand feet higher. 'Orbit' meant 'circle'. 'Vector' meant 'course', always followed by the number, as for example 'Vector 230', which meant 'fly on a course of 230 degrees'. 'Pancake' was the order to land, though pilots used the word to describe a squashing-down landing, the kind they had to make when the undercarriage had jammed.

On 1 September 1939 the Headquarters of the British Advanced Air Striking Force opened at Reims, a much easier place from which to attack the Germans than any home base was. The Force itself consisted of ten squadrons of Battles: 12, 15, 40, 88, 103, 105, 142, 150, 218, and 226. A week later, Hurricanes arrived: 1, 73, 85 and 87 Squadrons, and a week after that, on the 15th, the Air Component set up its Headquarters at Le Mans.

The Air Component presents any researcher with considerable difficulty. There is no doubt that it fought well and bravely, but, when it comes to detailed information, as the Air Ministry reports say with delightful ruefulness, researchers must, with regret, be referred to a spot impossible to determine at the bottom of the harbour of Boulogne. In the hasty business of getting personnel and aircraft away from France before the Germans caught up with them, many unit-records were burnt. The rest, including Headquarters papers, were piled up on a quay at Boulogne and subsequently shoved into the harbour, whether through lack of shipping or time or common sense no one knows.

The British zone of operations in France was carefully marked out. It lay between two lines of demarcation, from the French Seventh Army boundary which ran through Audenarde and Ghent to Antwerp and Nijmegen, and a line from Maulde through Duisberg to Paderborn. Of course, any flying over neutral territory was out of the question, so the Royal Air Force was strictly warned never to fly over the Low Countries unless, or until, these were dragged into war. If and when such flights were permitted, Bomber Command would be employed on strategic reconnaissance flights north of the Rivers Lek and Rhine as far east as Düsseldorf. In general Nijmegen– Duisberg was the eastern limit, meaning in practice not more than sixty miles east of any advancing German columns, and reconnaissance here was to be strategic and photographic, with emphasis on so-called sensitive points – the water-lines, which were the Rhine and Maas Rivers and the network of north Belgian canals, especially the Albert and the Dyle. Additional stress was laid upon the importance of points where roads running east and west crossed water running north and south. Aircraft crews must also note where the Belgian and Dutch forces were, whether any bridges and railways had been demolished or disrupted and if so where, any German-occupied airfields and the position of any

German anti-aircraft guns. All troop movements and concentrations, especially the movements of armoured columns, were to be reported at once.

Air reconnaissance was the principal source of information, and, considering criticisms made later, it is worth noting that the British were better equipped for this, in spite of their smaller numbers, than either the French or the Germans. The French had something like fifty reconnaissance aircraft, the Germans thirty-one. The Royal Air Force had sixty-four Blenheims and ninety Lysanders.

Bomber Command's primary commitment would be to co-operate with the French Army and Air Force. This meant that Bomber Command could be used either strategically or tactically. Strategically meant carrying the attack into German territory, against specified targets. Tactically meant going for German armed traffic moving into the Low Countries and France. The training programme for Bomber Command was based on these two types of attack.

But it was soon apparent that the Battles' heavy rate of loss proved that they could not penetrate into German territory by day. As a result, Bomber Command assumed that all available Blenheims would be employed in raids on the Ruhr, the Rhineland and the Saar. The French on the other hand assumed that only some of the Blenheims would go on such operations, because the rest would be kept for actions where land battles were in progress.

The formation in January 1940 of British Air Force in France Command helped to clarify these different points of view somewhat, but British aircraft would still have to operate, so to speak, 'on spec': for example, who could say whether the Germans were going to invade the Low Countries or mount their attack against France alone by way of the Maginot Line?

All these tentative plans and suggestions were accompanied by protracted Anglo-French discussions, but the only clear point to emerge was the disconcerting fact that the Royal Air Force was most unlikely to be given a free hand in France, or anything like a free hand. And of this Sir Hugh Dowding was well aware. It confirmed him in his determination not to throw all the forces at his disposal into Europe. In 1914 Kitchener had warned the War Cabinet not to throw away the small but magnificent British Army in the opening weeks of what he was certain would be a long war, but they had very nearly done it all the same. As far as Fighter Command was concerned, Dowding was not going to let such a thing happen again with all its calamitous consequences.

Of all places, the building most closely associated with the Royal Air Force in 1940 is Bentley Priory, headquarters of Fighter Command. Named after a small religious house of which no trace is left, the house stands on the highest hill in Middlesex, 500 feet above sea level. It belonged to the Marquess of Abercorn who entertained many celebrities there: at the time when Napoleon was exiled in Elba, the Prince Regent, Czar Alexander II of Russia, and King Frederick William III of Prussia came there to meet King Louis XVIII of France who was preparing to return to his own country. Sir Walter Scott revised the proofs of *Marmion* in a summerhouse in the garden. After the death of King William IV in 1837 his widow, Queen Adelaide, lived there (on a state pension of a hundred thousand pounds a year) and died there in 1849. The small room she died in is still preserved, with its plaster mouldings and ornate ceiling in light, often bright colours, and Queen Adelaide's gilt-framed looking-glass over the original chimney-piece.

The house is quietly attractive, built of brownish-grey stone in the Italianate style so popular in the nineteenth century, with a pillared porte-cochère at the front, and a typical narrow clock-tower topped by a neat little square slate roof. The graceful main staircase has metal lacework panels let in to the banister. Some of the rooms have encrusted plaster ceilings and one is domed. The south front, at the rear of the house, has large windows above the terrace and the formal Italian-style part of the garden, which then falls away downhill among its trees to give a magnificent view for miles, punctuated, dead centre, by Harrow Hill with its crowning spire. Dowding's office has this view, and a fine view is always therapeutic and tranquillising. His desk still stands there, though it is further from the windows than he placed it. The walls are hung with pictures of notables of the time connected with Fighter Command, including two photographs taken on a Royal visit, showing Dowding with the King and Queen in the gardens, the King, of course, wearing the uniform of a Marshal of the Royal Air Force. A framed copy of Dowding's famous 'minimum strength' letter hangs on the wall. There are albums of photographs and visitors' books on the table, and in a glass-topped case is a file containing photocopies of notes and memoranda written in Dowding's own hand in the summer and autumn of 1940. The furniture is plain and simple. Dowding was never ostentatious.

If there was one particular thing about the Royal Air Force that charmed the general public, it was their slang. After all, there are good-looking young men in becoming uniforms in all the Services. But the Royal Air Force's slang passed into common currency, and carries the flavour of the Forties with it still.

They called an aircraft a *crate*, or a *kite*. If one crash-landed, it was a *prang*, but it was also a *prang* if one's bombs or guns hit the target. If an aircraft had its undercarriage damaged so that it had to squash down on the airfield, it had *pancaked*. If it fell into the sea, it had *gone into the drink*. If it had been so badly damaged that it would have to be scrapped, it was a *write-off*.

If another airman was shot down, he had *got the chop* or *got the hammer*. If it was certain that he was dead, he had *bought it* – though equally the words '*I've bought it that time*' could mean 'Well, I asked for that'. To *strafe* was to machine-gun something: troops on the Dunkirk beaches were *strafed*. It was a German borrowing and pronounced to rhyme with 'half'. Flying on observation or patrol was called *stooging around*. The rear gunner was the *tail-end stooge* or, more often, the *tail-end Charlie*.

If someone was expected to arrive that day, a guest, a visiting dignitary, a girl friend, people would ask '*What's the ETA?*' (the estimated time of arrival). If the person were late, or if someone took a moment to see the point of a remark, that was DA (delayed action). A remark of warm approval was '*I care for that*'. Conversely strong disapproval was shown by '*I don't care for that*'.

A *flap* was any kind of collective hustle or anxiety: '*There's a flap on*', or, to a worried colleague, '*Don't get in a flap*'.

19

Information was *gen*. *Pukka gen* was absolutely definite information. *Ropey* meant much the same as today's 'tatty', and could apply to objects or to people, as in '*He's rather a ropey type*'. *Type* was a person, usually a man: *shocking type* might be seriously meant, but rather more often was '*not a bad chap*'. If someone expected a rebuke, a scolding, or a criticism, a friend would tell him '*They're going to tear you off a strip*'.

Clot was 'silly blighter'. *Get cracking*, or, later, *get weaving*, both still in use, meant 'hurry up', 'get moving' or 'jump to it'. To *get screechers* meant to have quite a lot to drink. '*This'll shake you*' meant 'this will surprise you', sometimes for added emphasis given as '*This'll shake you rigid*'. *Shooting a line* was talking big, boasting, making an impression on a girl ('*I must shoot her a terrific line*'), though sometimes it could simply mean 'telling a string of lies'.

Wizard, which was enthusiastically taken up in schools, meant marvellous. Sometimes, in praise of a particularly fine exploit, the phrase was *wizard show*, though more often it was simply *good show*. Other phrases of approval were *bang on* and *spot on*.

And everybody adopted the expression 'I've had it' or 'You've had it', which meant precisely the opposite. 'Did you have a bath?' 'Oh, I had it all right – no hot water'. The widespread use of *you've had it* meaning you've missed it (bus, train) or we've sold out (pencils, cakes) especially bewildered foreigners.

But perhaps two expressions, in the way they were used, summed up the wartime Royal Air Force best of all. '*I was shot down in flames*' (sometimes with the words *Smoke pouring from the starboard engine* added) meant 'I've had a difference of opinion with my girl'. On the other hand a harrowing and highly dangerous sortie would be referred to as *quite a party*.

2

Backdrop

The greatest of all the achievements of the air service is that in a very few years, under the hammer of war, it has fashioned and welded its tradition, and has made it sure. Critics who speak of what they have not felt and do not know have sometimes blamed the air service because, being young, it has not the decorum of age . . . To see him [the pilot] at his best they would have to accompany him, through the storm of anti-aircraft guns, into those fields of air where every moment brings some new trial of the quickness of his brain and the steadiness of his nerve.

Walter Raleigh

In August 1914 a Staff Officer at Maubeuge telephoned the British GHQ, saying plaintively: 'I've got some fellows here who call themselves an Aircraft Park. What on earth am I supposed to do with them?' In fact these newcomers were the Second, Third, Fourth and Fifth Squadrons of the Royal Flying Corps, freshly arrived in France, the first national air force ever to go overseas. At first the squadrons were employed merely in aerial reconnaissance, and they soon found that ground troops, unused to aircraft, had an alarming habit of shooting at any they saw. The first wartime air reconnaissance in history took placed on Wednesday 19 August. Two aircraft, a Blériot and a BE (Blériot Experimental), with pilots only, carrying no observers, took off from Maubeuge at nine o'clock in the morning with orders to find the German Army. Lieutenant Mapplebeck in the BE, told to fly north, found the skies cloudy, and, as his maps were on a scale of 1:1,000,000, it is perhaps hardly surprising that he flew over the city of Brussels without recognising it. In the Blériot Captain Philippe Joubert de la Ferté, famous a war later as Air Chief Marshal Sir Philip Joubert, who had been told to fly west, wandered about, as he put it, without seeing anything helpful. In those days it was thought very bad form to come down to ask the way, but, when he saw a large town flying Belgian flags, he landed on the barracks parade-ground, where the garrison told him he was at Tournai and gave him an excellent luncheon. He took off again, cruised about, recognised Bruges, and landed at Courtrai, where the suspicious local police threatened to put him in jail. A visiting Ulster linen manufacturer spoke up for him, identifying his plane as British, and the police, now all smiles, gave him plenty of petrol and told him the way back to Maubeuge. He and Mapplebeck arrived there in the late afternoon, neither of them having set eyes on a German. They could only say, more or less, where the Germans were not.

From this modest, tentative start the Junior Service grew into a force capable of engaging German aircraft, among them the Richthofen Circus, as that sensational group came to be called. Yet perhaps because of the make-it-up-as-you-go-along nature of its first appearance on the international military scene, the Royal Air Force had a highly individual style which it never lost. It always, so to speak, sat lightly in the saddle: its members had a misleadingly casual air, a strong vein of improvisation and an equally strong vein of irreverence, a habit of wearing their caps tilted and of looking anyone straight in the eye. In their own special language, manner and skills, they had their own glamour, making them in many ways the most glamorous of the three Services in the War of 1939–1945.

Partly this arose out of their particular conditions of battle. In the Army all men were involved in (for example) the advance to attack, moving forward as part of a vast mass, camping out where they halted, then moving on, or perhaps back, from that point. In the Royal Navy the men lived and fought in their ships, and all ranks were equally committed to battle. But in the Royal Air Force the actual fighting was done by comparatively small numbers of officers, warrant officers and sergeants: for every seven men in combat there were forty ground staff to make combat possible, embodying a wide range of skills, and each sortie took off from and returned to base. Certainly the ground staff, their airfields and equipment, were often under attack themselves, but it was clear from the first that (like the other two Services) theirs was a fighting force that operated in a unique way.

Naturally it takes time for the full potential of an air force to be fully realised. When realisation in Britain began, it had an effect which surprises us now, but seemed logical at the time. Until 1939 the War of 1914–1918 was still, justifiably, called the Great War, and it left such scars that strong belief in, and clamour for, disarmament increasingly existed. The limited bomb-attacks on civilians in the Great War frightened many in authority, not so much because of the casualties (a drop in the ocean compared with the military casualties at the Front) as because of the authorities' dread of the panic and loss of morale that bombing seemed certain to produce. 'Avoid war at all costs' therefore made sense, and 'appeasement' was a perfectly honourable word. Successive governments, debating armament-cuts, always began with the Royal Air Force. Their views were strengthened in 1932 by the outbreak of war between China and Japan, from which the cinema news reels, stressing bombing-raids on cities, were horrifying, prompting Stanley Baldwin to tell the House of Commons on 10 November in that year that 'the bomber will always get through'. In the tenser atmosphere of 1936 the release of the film Things To Come, which opened with a sudden declaration of war instantly followed by vast waves of enemy bombers blasting London (called 'Everytown' in the film, but no matter) to rubble, reinforced these fears. It is, incidentally, an interesting point that, when Neville Chamberlain broadcast the British declaration of war on the morning of Sunday 3 September, 1939, and the air raid sirens were tested just as he finished speaking, thousands of people thought: 'Things To Come' – this is it'. Only it wasn't.

Another factor that operated in favour of disarmament was the considerable Parliamentary representation of businessmen, who, if they had to spend taxpayers' money, naturally preferred to spend it on trade rather than on the armed forces. Chamberlain himself was one such.

It was remarkably late in the day when British officials in high places awoke to the fact of German re-armament, or at any rate to its implications. Forbidding Germany to re-arm had been a key principle of the Treaty of Versailles in 1919. Germany could have a standing army of one hundred thousand, but no tanks, big guns, or aircraft. Most governments seem to have taken it for granted that Germany was keeping to this (until it was too late). But Germany had two distinct advantages unsuspected for years. She had lost the Great War, therefore her Army was no longer burdened with out-of-date theories or equipment. Neither had brought victory in 1918: both could be scrapped with hardly a backward look. And there was the Army Commander-in-Chief.

Colonel-General Hans von Seeckt had been Chief of Staff to General Mackensen on the Eastern Front where in 1915 his best-known exploit had been a spectacular breakthrough at Gorlice. With his stern bearing and fashionable monocle he looked the archetypal Prussian Officer, but his appearance concealed a marked capacity for broad and flexible ideas. He became Commander-in-Chief in the immediate aftermath of defeat, determined to provide what he saw as the antidote to Versailles' poison, by which he meant the disarmament clauses, and to lay the groundwork of a future top quality German Army. The victorious Allies had demanded a cut of twenty thousand German Army Officers: von Seeckt of course complied, but he made certain that those remaining were a true élite, and of the permitted hundred thousand, forty thousand were Non-Commissioned Officers of proper 'officer material'. He wanted to keep going the traditional values of the old German Army, but he encouraged better inter-rank relations, easier comradeship and a thoroughly professional attitude.

As tanks were forbidden, until 1932 only dummy ones, usually wooden and propelled on bicycle-wheels, were seen at manoeuvres. Small armoured vehicles with revolving turrets were permitted, somewhat reluctantly, after that, and could not carry guns, but they were of the greatest use in training all the same. No vehicles with tracks were allowed, but the Germans evolved armoured cars with eight wheels, which easily became the excellent reconnaissance light eight-wheelers of the later War. Von Seeckt also encouraged the use of motor-cycles, another valuable element in later attacks. He made everyone study the mistakes of the past, so that new training methods and principles could develop, and the old training manuals were rewritten.

But as early as 1923 von Seeckt was convinced that a German Air Force must be built up, and he started to plan what he called 'an Air Force skeleton' inside the German Army such as it was, in such a way that the skeleton could not be discovered or deduced from outside. He was greatly helped by the fact that, of all military forces, air power is the hardest to assess or measure. Civil aviation, to which no one had the slightest objection, needed its factories, airfields and training-grounds, affording plenty of camouflage for military preparations. The result was that Hitler found his desired short cut ready to his hand, as his Luftwaffe gained equality with the air forces of France and Britain and then outstripped them, making possible not only the rapid conquest of Poland but the great breakthrough in the West.

23

One young man who learnt from von Seeckt was Staff Captain Heinz Guderian, who in 1922 at the age of thirty-four was put on the Staff of German Army Motor Transport. He had been an Intelligence Officer at the Crown Prince's Headquarters in the Great War, stationed at Verdun in 1916. Like so many young men on both sides, he was so sickened by the waste of lives there that he was convinced no such huge full-scale attacks should ever again be a part of warfare: any future conflicts should aim for quick attacks with a minimum of casualties. (Two notable British examples of this thinking, who like Guderian led armies with singular success in the later war, were Bernard Law Montgomery and Harold Rupert Leofric George Alexander.) Guderian had specialised in signals, and his appointment to Motor Transport introduced him to mechanised warfare. He imbibed not only von Seeckt's theories but also those of Basil Liddell Hart and other British military tacticians. When he was picked to assist Lieutenant-Colonel von Brauchitsch on co-ordinated exercises using motorised troops and aircraft, and then when he was asked to lecture troops on military history and strategy, his ideas developed to the point where, in 1929, he had grasped the importance of making properly integrated armoured divisions as a spearhead instead of, as formerly, using tanks to follow up infantry. He employed a translator at his own expense to translate Liddell Hart's published articles as soon as they appeared in English periodicals, and in 1937 produced a book entitled *Achtung – Panzer!*

As Germany had used only a handful of tanks in the Great War, Guderian drew his analyses from Allied examples, taking the British as the more practical, as they did not tie their tanks to infantry-pace as the French did. Both, however, had, he thought, failed to understand the tanks' full potential. What tanks should do included attacking in massive concentrations, at speed and in depth, and, not content with breaking the enemy line, must break right through it, thereby putting out of action the enemy reserves, batteries, supply-lines and Staff positions. Therefore there must be well-designed fast-moving tanks armed with machine-guns as well as cannon, and armoured strongly enough to protect themselves, yet not so heavily that they would sacrifice the essential speed and mobility. Close behind would come motorised troops and mobile anti-tank guns which would follow up the spearhead and guard its flanks. Essential to success was surprise: which led him in time to think of the way to achieve it, by sending the Luftwaffe in first, especially the dive-bombers, to catch the enemy unawares. The follow-up to the breakthrough would need only comparatively slender Panzer forces. To achieve the complete knock-out blow would mean attacking in width as well as in depth, to avoid being outflanked. And it must be done across the right kind of ground. So in his book he was really giving the plan he would so successfully put into practice three years later. – The book was not translated into either English or French, and as far as anyone knows its ideas were not considered by any senior military people in either country, despite the fact that articles about them had appeared in widely distributed magazines. One person who did pay attention, and with warm approval, was Hitler, who had said in 1933 that another European war could not have the prolonged struggle and fixed deadlock with huge casualty figures on both sides of the Great War, which he called 'a degenerate form of war'. By the end of 1938 Guderian was a full General and appointed Chief of Mobile Troops.

As for the French, while many foreigners still thought of the French Army as the greatest in Europe, and recalled the centuries of success and tradition that lay behind it (summed up in the French term *la gloire*), in fact French military affairs were bedevilled as never before. And not only military affairs. The ill-starred Third Republic appeared to change governments every few weeks, and jokes proliferated of the 'oh, yes, he was Minister of the Interior for ten minutes in 1934' type. Great Britain was up against government reluctance to spend public money on arms: France was far worse off, for each change of ministry meant change of programme, orders placed by one being altered or cancelled whether production had started or not. More: the French were deeply embittered by the terrible losses they had suffered in the Great War, embittered all the more deeply because their population was markedly lower than that of Germany. Victory in 1918 seemed a small, sour fruit to have been purchased at such cost. So the French reacted into a kind of despairing frivolity, often cynical, with undertones of 'what's the use?' Germany, it is true, had been through a worse Depression than France had, and had likewise reacted into frivolity in the Twenties, when Berlin was the place foreigners went to for a thrill: but Hitler had stopped all that, and his new arms industry had cut unemployment, new recruits to the armed forces finishing it off. Bismarck had said that a generation that has taken a beating is always followed by a generation that gives one, and the French, beaten in 1870, had won in 1918, but the taste of victory was not sweet. Ahead of much of Europe, though few would let themselves believe anything so unpalatable, they sensed that a prolonged modern war punishes victor and vanquished alike.

Between the Wars, the French had spent millions of francs building the Maginot Line, a tremendous fortification stretching the length of the Franco-German frontier. This, though impregnable as it was claimed to be, left unaltered the eternal geographic fact that the easiest way for Germany to invade France is by way of Belgium, where dozens of old battlefields and hundreds of military cemeteries testify to centuries of struggle, most clearly of course to the efforts of 1914–1918. Germany could afford to ignore the Maginot Line, and did so, stationing only nineteen Army divisions along it, whereas the French on their side had fifty-nine divisions. This meant that the French had fewer men to put where they would really be needed, further north. So in fact the Germans actually profited far more than the French from that mighty fortification.

Despite all setbacks, cuts and delays, and most fortunately as it turned out, two Chiefs of the British Air Staff had been working away unobtrusively to make the Royal Air Force better prepared for war. Marshal of the Royal Air Force Sir Edward Ellington between 1933 and 1937, and his successor, Air Chief Marshal Sir Cyril Newall, set various projects in motion. Among these were the Royal Air Force Volunteer Reserve, which collected adherents from the beginning, the making of new airfields, the setting-up of the four Commands – Training Command, Coastal Command, Bomber Command, Fighter Command – and the production of invaluable new aircraft. It was Ellington and Newall, with their designers and helpers, who developed the Short Stirling and Avro Manchester which led to the Handley Page Halifax and Avro Lancaster bombers, and who were all-important in bringing into being the two matchless fighters, the Hawker Hurricane and the Supermarine Spitfire. Not only that: they made possible that weapon beyond price, Radio Direction Finding, better known as Radar. At every step they were hampered by very different groups of people: the dedicated disarmers, the alarm-spreaders who thought nothing could stop the bomber, and the cheeseparing and dubious politicians. But despite all that it was Ellington's and Newall's insight and quiet persistence that had the Royal Air Force (barely) ready to go to war in 1939, and able (but only just) to win the Battle of Britain in 1940.

One completely unexpected thing that probably made all the difference was 'the phony war'. Far from the war starting with a devastating fleet of enemy bombers darkening the English sky, there was the curious period of seven months, from September 1939 to April 1940, when hardly anything seemed to be happening at all. Poland had been crushed in twenty-eight days: whereupon any Polish Air Force personnel who could escape came to Britain, in due course contributing their own blend of gallantry and intransigence to the war effort. It is essential to say 'in due course'. They arrived anxious above all things to carry on fighting. It was frustrating for pilots with, say, more than 2,000 hours' flying behind them to have to wait until they knew enough English to make sense of English instructions and information. But there was no help for it. Few Britons spoke reasonable French, and air speed indicators were marked in feet, not the familiar metres. Also, the Poles had never flown with retractable undercarriages. The Northolt Station Commander, after seeing too many accidents, firmly ordered all the Poles grounded until their English was workable. Of course they resented the delay, but they could understand the reasons for it – and they certainly made up for it later. The Polish War Memorial, crowned with wings, stands as a familiar traffic landmark today overlooking the A40 at the south-east corner of Northolt airfield. But, apart from the Royal Navy's famous double exploit, the Battle of the River Plate and the successful pursuit of the *Altmark*, there seemed absolutely nothing special to write home about. It was a strange, twilit interval. But it gave the Royal Air Force a breathing-space.

If a breathing-space was needed, a fresh appraisal certainly was. During the two years before the War there had been strong differences of opinion between the Air Staff and the Commanders-in-Chief of both Bomber and Fighter Commands. Until about 1937 the official belief seemed to be that Bomber Command provided a deterrent by its very existence, and only then did anyone in authority begin to consider general strategy and actual tactics in a practical way, drawing up theoretical battle plans and working out orders suitable for the men who would have to do any fighting there was. Of the forty-nine bomber squadrons of 1938, twenty-four consisted of obsolescent aircraft: Fairey Battles, Handley Page Harrows, and Vickers Wellesleys. The other twenty-five squadrons, of Bristol Blenheims and Armstrong-Whitworth Whitleys, were better, but not brilliant: the Blenheims' range was too limited and the Whitley, a tough old workhorse, was reliable indeed, giving useful service until 1943, but there were only nine squadrons of them. The Air Staff told Bomber Command that its war priorities should be to attack three main objectives: the German Air Force and its industrial plant, German rail, road and water routes leading to the West, and the Ruhr heavy industry. These objectives were all questioned by the Commander-in-Chief.

He was Air Chief Marshal Sir Edgar Ludlow-Hewitt, then fifty years old, who had been appointed on 12 September 1937. He had made a precise inspection of every part of his Command, and had found many faults which his lively, enthusiastic, generally well-trained airmen were struggling valiantly to overcome. Bomber Command was dangerously vulnerable. It could operate only in good weather, and, Ludlow-Hewitt said bluntly, it was not at all ready for war. Many improvements were wanted at once, and he placed special emphasis on two of them: all-weather, round-the-clock navigational practice, and efficient air-crew training. The Flying Schools were excellent, but could not supply enough men, so the squadrons had to do most of the training themselves. Therefore the proper navigational equipment, and plenty of it, was essential. After all, Bomber Command would have to make long flights over enemy territory to find their targets; Civil Aviation could, and did, fly in all weathers by day and night with excellent instruments and reliable ground control, so the least that Bomber Command should be able to expect was the same. But another problem was that not until then had the Air Staff regarded air-crew as a full-time job, apart from the pilot, and, with the new bombers requiring crews of six or seven, the sooner each crew was recognised and trained as a fighting unit, working as a team and accustomed to it, the better. Ludlow-Hewitt did his best, unweariedly pressing for improvements, but he had to struggle against Treasury parsimony on one hand and Air Staff reluctance to admit they had guessed wrong on the other. This meant that as late as the summer of 1939 almost half his bomber crews could not be sure of finding a given target even when unopposed in daylight. Finding a target was not easy at the best of times, and to be sure of hitting it was hard, while British bombs were of poor quality, many indeed being leftovers from the previous War, often failing to go off, often doing little damage when they did. For a long time dive-bombing was believed impossible (until the Germans proved the contrary), so low-level attacks were taught. These, naturally, were much riskier, exposing the aircraft to all the dangers of anti-aircraft fire and barrage balloons as well as to the hazards of flying low over hills, radio masts, tall buildings. One crew-member particularly at risk was the isolated rear-gunner, who was inadequately trained and equipped to face the full eight-gun attack of the new fighter planes. It was not, in fact, until October 1940 that the Central Gunnery School Ludlow-Hewitt had been asking for was set up, when the pressures of war had pushed home the force of his arguments unanswerably. The Official History summed up Bomber Command's position in September 1939 by saying simply that it was in no fit state to get into enemy territory by day or to find its target area by night.

On 10 November 1938 the Secretary of State for Air, Sir Kingsley Wood, told the House of Commons of a new plan, to be completed by the end of March 1942, to increase the number of Royal Air Force squadrons to 163, eighty-five of them for Bomber Command and fifty for Fighter Command. Sir Kingsley said that Fighter Command was to have priority, as it was the force that would have to meet the invading bombers in the air – which rebutted, six years to the day after it was spoken, Baldwin's phrase 'the bomber will always get through'. This change of attitude had come about because of the production of the eight-gun fighter and the growth of Radar, and now fighters were being built faster than anyone had expected, supplying thirty-nine squadrons by August 1939 – though by then it was clear that the remaining eleven, and a good many more, were needed at once, never mind waiting until 1942.

We shall return to Fighter Command in a moment. First we must take a quick look at the opposition.

Everyone concerned in Germany agreed that the Luftwaffe must be built up to make possible quick victories in short campaigns. Speed was of the essence. Therefore from 1936 the policy was to build light and medium bombers rather than the big heavyweights which took much more material and labour, and to concentrate on a few types of aircraft, not a wide variety. The Luftwaffe was always treated as part of the Army – its officers had Army rank – and its duties were to take the offensive, to open the way for the Army and to back it up as required. This mode of operations would win the Battle of France, but lose the Battle of Britain.

The main types of Luftwaffe aircraft were, therefore, three Junkers, the 87, the 88, and the invaluable old workhorse, the transport 52, which had revealed its value in Spain, carrying fuel, spare parts and bombs rapidly from one airfield to another; the Dornier 17, referred to as the Flying Pencil because of its slim shape; the Heinkel 111; and the two Messerschmidts, the 110 'destroyer' (which was found far too vulnerable in practice) and the excellent 109. This, in its version described as the BF 109 E, is rightly considered one of the greatest combat aircraft in history. It was formidably armed, with two 20-mm cannon in the wings and two 7.9-mm machine-guns in the fuselage. Its Daimler-Benz engine could achieve 348mph at 14,560 feet and a climbing rate of 30,000 feet a minute. The Royal Air Force came to regard it with the respect it deserved.

But perhaps the aircraft that proved the most spectacular, in the early stages of the War at any rate, was the Junkers 87 in its rôle as dive-bomber. This was ironical as by 1940 it was thought to be on its way out. It had first shown its power when a few of them were flown with the Condor Legion in Spain, whereupon German military opinion divided, more senior officers having misgivings while others hailed the Junkers 87 as a war-winning phenomenon. One devotee was Ernst Udet, former flying ace of the previous war, now Director-General of Luftwaffe Equipment, and he promoted the Stuka, a word that very soon had dramatic overtones. It was the slang version of *Sturzkampfflugzeug*, and it climbed high into the sky, levelled out, then, at the right distance from the target, hurtled down like the stoop of a falcon, but with a terrifying screeching noise. This came from the siren fitted on the fixed undercarriage, which Udet called the trumpet of Jericho, and, as it screamed down with claws extended, or so it appeared, it certainly created panic, but it was relatively slow and would fall victim to British fighters later at much too costly a rate. Its value in the Battle of France was as mobile artillery, moving much faster than the big guns to crucial attack-points, fully justified in the spring of 1940 as it had been in Poland. Its devotees found it a well-built machine, strong, easy to handle and a delight to fly, almost uncannily accurate on its target and quick in manoeuvre. Its detractors said it was vulnerable because its cruising speed was only 175 mph, easy prey to a good fighter plane. It would seem that the critics had prevailed, for it was scheduled for withdrawal

Junkers JU-87 (Stuka).

by the end of 1939. But as things turned out it was considered worth its weight in gold in the Western assault.

Luftwaffe officials were delighted to display to visiting dignitaries their impressive show of air power, whether it was real or still a cardboard front, as the effect was so striking. The French Chief of the Air Staff, General Vuillemin, with his second-in-command General d'Astier de la Vigerie, went to Germany in August 1938, and found the experience, as he put it, 'shattering'. Reporting back to the French Foreign Minister, Georges Bonnet, he said that if war came there would not be a French plane left after a couple of weeks. Bonnet, the epitome of French appeasement, was more set in his attitude than ever.

It was in 1938 that, with the German takeover of Austria, there were now 76 million Germans to 42 million French.

Despite the promise of more squadrons, problems still troubled Fighter Command. Its Commander-in-Chief, taking office three days before the Spanish Civil War opened, arrived quietly and alone, on the stroke of nine on the morning of 14 July 1936 at his Headquarters, Bentley Priory at Stanmore. (When he was rather belatedly raised to the Peerage in 1943 it was as Baron Dowding of Bentley Priory.) That first day he was Air Chief Marshal Sir Hugh Caswall Tremenheere Dowding, aged fifty-four. Along with two others who were to achieve military distinction, Wavell and Portal, he had been educated at Winchester, where the two guiding doctrines of service to one's country and good manners formed his philosophy of life. A man of unflinching logic and reason, together with a degree of foresight that astonishes even yet, he found himself at once mistrustful of the theories suggested by the Air Staff. For example, they had divided the country into four defence zones, from each of which fighter squadrons could be summoned to the aid of any other. Dowding, who knew all about aircraft range and speed, saw instantly how impractical this would be. Who could imagine fighters holding bombers at bay over London long enough for (say) Scottish-based squadrons to join them? It was certain that the south-east of England would be the foremost enemy target. Dowding therefore abolished the zones, put the main fighter strength in the South and reduced it through the Midlands to the lightest force in the North. On another occasion he suggested that Hurricanes and Spitfires ought to have their windscreens of bullet-proof glass, which struck the Air Staff members present as comic. When they stopped laughing he simply said that if Chicago gangsters could have bullet-proof glass he saw no reason why his pilots should not have it too. He was always sensitive about casualties: even after 'good' days of battle he never forgot the men who had died. From his punctilious, courteous manner and his habit of keeping his papers in apple-pie order he was nicknamed Stuffy by his Staff, but it was a nickname carrying undertones of real affection as well as deep respect.

His main preoccupation was to build up as formidable a fighting force as possible. He told the Air Staff that he must have every one of the squadrons which they had finally decided were needed to meet the expected two thousand German bombers, if, as he put it, Germany occupied the Low Countries and thus had south-east England within range. He set these forty-six squadrons as his absolute minimum requirement. By the summer of 1939, as we have seen, he had thirty-nine. But there were threats even to these. He was asked for four to protect East Coast convoys (Coastal Command, low in numbers and with out-of-date aircraft, Ansons, London, Stranraer and Sunderland flying-boats, Hudsons, and twenty-year-old Vildebeest torpedo-bombers, could not provide proper protection), two to defend the Home Fleet at Scapa Flow, and one for Northern Ireland. Regretfully but firmly he refused.

But then came a demand impossible to refuse. The British Expeditionary Force going to France must have air cover. Dowding was too loyal, and too honest, to deny that the only possible planes for this purpose must be the best, which meant Hurricanes. So four precious squadrons were earmarked for France, which reduced Dowding to thirty-five and, moreover, filled him with the natural worries felt by any Commander part of whose force is going to be subject to the needs and even the orders of an Ally. Stubbornly refusing further demands, he went on asking for more Hurricanes and Spitfires. His reasoning was sound: real fighter strength would deter an enemy, while moderate fighter strength would not, and weak fighter force would positively invite attack. This would not only destroy Fighter Command but would allow enemy bombs to wipe out most, perhaps all, of Britain's production centres, civil and military. Home Defence, said Dowding, must take precedence over everything else, as the life of the nation rested upon two things, the Royal Navy and Fighter Command. He repeated this at every crucial moment.

During the 'phony war' the Royal Air Force had time to learn many important lessons. The first was the absolute necessity to make aircraft radio reliable at once. The earliest reconnaissance flights of the War, on 3 and 4 September, had to be reported by the pilots in person on return to base, as what they had said over the radio at the time had not been heard. This was simply not good enough. The second lesson was that attacking warships head-on was more practical than to attack broadside, as head-on presented the attacker with the full length of the ship. Air-crews learnt that the Wellington bombers' rear turrets, with their two guns, could hold off the Messerschmidts and, even if they did get close in, it took a lot of firing to destroy, or even seriously disable, a Wellington. They found that Wellingtons flying in close formation were more formidable and less likely to be put out of action than those flying in loose formation. (It would take some time for them to discover that the opposite held true of fighters.) It ought to have been obvious all along, but soon was, that squadrons which had flown together managed better than those which had not, and – a crucial point – that daylight operations cost far more than night-flying in aircraft missing, destroyed or disabled. Valuable night-flying practice, so urgently needed, was gained through the derided leaflet-dropping sorties, which were really a pretext for reconnaissance. Air-crews were told to study the ground they were flying over, to observe any movements of enemy transport by land and water, airfield activity, blackout conditions, and to note the position and quality of searchlights and anti-aircraft fire. All this taught the air-crews much, and provided quantities of information much of which was helpful later in the War.

These flights were made in the reliable old Whitleys, which, as the winter came on, and it was the coldest winter in Europe for forty-five years, subjected air-crews to hardships hitherto unimagined. Reports exist of Whitleys with inches of ice on their wings or sticking out of the engine-cowlings, causing uncontrollable drops of the aircraft through thousands of feet of air, and, even without these hazards, the Whitleys were so cold that men went numb, and sometimes even fainted or collapsed.

The first night-bombing raid took place in mid-March with fifty aircraft, thirty Whitleys and twenty Hampdens, forty-three of which located and attacked the sea-plane base on the island of Sylt, just off the German coast close to the Danish border. The attack did little damage, which served to emphasise the still unsatisfactory performance of navigational aids. It was a lowering reflection for Ludlow-Hewitt to retire on. On 3 April he became Inspector-General of the Royal Air Force. His successor, Marshal of the Royal Air Force Sir Arthur 'Bomber' Harris, described him as the most brilliant officer he ever met and the finest of Commanders, and added that, as Inspector-General, Ludlow-Hewitt was highly influential in organisation, design, and production, all of the greatest value to the Service. Sir John Slessor, who agreed with all this, said that in his time as Inspector-General Ludlow-Hewitt put in some 800 flying hours in his own aircraft during the War, which was pretty good for a man not far off sixty.

All this time, Fighter Command had been concentrating on training, welcoming each new Hurricane or Spitfire and new recruit, while Dowding went relentlessly on asking for aircraft. And Coastal Command, the poor relation of the Royal Air Force as it too often felt itself to be, had been learning to manage better, and was by now achieving a quite notable rate of success in destroying mines scattered by the German Navy in British coastal waters.

True to her long-standing and well-justified fear of invasion, Russia had taken steps to guard her western borders. During the autumn of 1939 she announced that she was prepared to take over military control of the Baltic states. Latvia, Lithuania and Estonia accepted this without a fight; Finland refused. Russia was ill-prepared for war, especially a winter war. Nevertheless Russian troops crossed the border into Finland. The Finns resisted bravely for more than a hundred days, which as much as anything gave the Western Powers, whether combatant or neutral, a firm belief that Russia was weak. As late as June 1941, on the eve of his invasion of the Soviet Union, Hitler declared that 'you have only to kick the front door and the whole house will fall down', and many sensible and otherwise well-informed people feared, or hoped, that he was probably right.

The invasion of Finland stirred Great Britain and France first to admiration and sympathy and then to make plans to help the Finns. An Allied Expeditionary Force began to make ready. In February 1940 the German ship Altmark, carrying some three hundred men of the Royal Navy captured at the River Plate, was followed into Norwegian waters by Captain Philip Vian in HMS Cossack, from which a boarding-party rescued the prisoners. By the beginning of March the Expeditionary Force was ready, but the Finns, hopelessly outnumbered, made peace with the Russians. Feeling guilty over their failure to help Finland as they had failed to help Poland, the British in high places thought that at least a gesture should be made. So they held the Expeditionary Force in readiness, and planned to lay mines off the coast of Norway. These movements in or towards the North Sea played a part in shaping Hitler's decision to invade Norway.

But we must return to September 1939. During the 'phony war' the British and the French wondered, in a vague way when it came to the general population, why nothing was happening. But they wondered with a difference. Many – too many – French asked: 'What are we waiting for? Surely there'll be a truce now'. The British asked: 'When's he going to move? What's he waiting for?'

Hitler had not wanted to wait. Poland surrendered on 27 September, and at five in the afternoon of that day he told his senior Commanders that now he had nothing to worry about in the East so he could launch the attack in the West, and at once, going by way of Belgium and Maastricht. Could they be ready to start on 25 November?

A chorus of horrified protests met this. One officer's murmur of 'lunacy' went unheard, but the other comments were. Impossible to be ready by then – too many tanks from Poland in the repair-shops – equipment short – November weather not good for flying. No, said Hitler, November it must be, so draw up plans at once.

The first plan for Deployment Directive Yellow, as it was obscurely called, was not a good one (they all admitted this) and led to arguments. Hitler startled them afresh by suddenly setting the attack-date forward to 12 November. More discussion. More canvassing of opinions. On 5 November, at another meeting with Hitler, General Heinrich von Brauchitsch opened the proceedings. Outwardly he was a very correct, quiet officer, inwardly a most intelligent and sensitive man who hated loud wrangling.

He had recently toured Army units and every Commanding Officer had reported that his men were nothing like ready. It was also, he added, important never to underestimate the French. Hitler interrupted him, saying he held quite different views. The French were all for peace and good living, and had been plagued by political quarrels for years, their Army was brave and well trained, but lacked the will to fight. Von Brauchitsch tried to go on, but Hitler exploded: why reproach our Army? You and the other Commanders are disloyal, go away and leave it to Keitel, he will move our troops up ready for the 12th. Hitler was sure (as curiously enough Churchill later was) that all too often Commanders will only say what they are afraid of, not what they know they can do. Luckily for Hitler, the weather broke two days later, and the attack was put off: as it was to be put off twenty-eight more times.

On 15 November two officers arrived from Poland to take command of Army Group A at Koblenz. One was Colonel-General Gerd von Rundstedt, aged nearly sixty-four, who had been called out of retirement to serve in Poland. His family was military: one at least of them had fought in every war the Prussian Army had taken part in for almost two centuries. He looked stolid, but was quick to appreciate situations, accomplished in tactics, admired by his men, and far too wise to ignore good advice or ideas wherever they came from. Not showy, he preferred to wear his Honorary Colonel of Infantry jacket rather than that of his rank, first as General then as Field-Marshal. He co-operated well with his Chief of Staff who arrived with him, General Erich von Manstein, aged fifty-two, who, he thought rightly, had vision. Von Manstein, like Guderian, had been at Verdun, and he too had realised that wars were not won by Verdun means. He had seen the Directive Yellow plan, and spotted every one of its flaws. A tall, hawk-faced, chilly man, he was known to be outstanding in dealing with large troop formations, and, leaving aside the doubtful morality of invading a neutral country, he was adamant that to invade Belgium was only worth doing if it proved truly decisive. Any attack should aim at cutting off the Allies and bottling them up, preferably towards the Channel coast. Von Manstein embodied his ideas in a paper which von Rundstedt forwarded to General Franz Halder, von Brauchitsch's second-in-command. Halder was also a quick thinker, sensible, precise, and that rare thing among German Commanders, a Bavarian Catholic. Of the many generals who hoped to get rid of Hitler somehow, Halder was in a particular dilemma: a loyal officer, an honourable man, vowed to obedience to his Supreme Commander, he had a Christian conscience which prohibited him from taking part in a violent coup. He read von Manstein's paper and decided that Hitler had better not be bothered with it just then. Von Manstein sent further papers, expanding his plan so that it concentrated more and more on the southern Meuse with a direct breakthrough to Sédan.

With a neatness of timing not often found in history, on the day von Manstein arrived at Koblenz Hitler, at another meeting with his Commanders, suggested, almost as a throwaway line, whether it was not possible to concentrate the attack on the southern part of the Meuse only. That would make it possible to cut off the enemy. He drew a red pencil line on the map south of Namur towards the French coast, by way of Sédan, and said: Go and think it over.

Von Manstein's paper was given to von Brauchitsch on 21 November when he visited Koblenz. Three weeks before, Hitler had told General Alfred Jodl that he had 'a new idea' – to attack through the Ardennes, cross the Meuse fifty miles south of Namur and strike at Sédan. The French had maintained for a long time, as a kind of military Holy Writ, that no army could pass the Ardennes: one distinguished general had dismissed it as impossible in the Great War (he was Philippe Pétain, hero of Verdun), and the German High Command, still picturing the French Army as it had been then, accepted that belief. Hitler had not argued, but he had not forgotten either.

In Berlin, on 23 November, Hitler summoned all the senior officers of the three Services, 180 men, to the Chancellery for one of his celebrated harangues. All this hesitation, all these postponements of Der Tag, must cease. Were they too cowardly to fight? Their soldiers were not. Well led, the Army could do anything. The Commanders left silently. Von Brauchitsch offered his resignation. Hitler refused it: 'Like any soldier, you have your duty to do'. The scolding had its effect: from that moment the Commanders were far readier to consider plans in a practical way.

Von Manstein invited Guderian to Koblenz, laid his plans before him, and from Guderian's comments realised for the first time how the Panzers must be the key. He promptly worked out fresh memoranda for Halder, who in effect told him to shut up and go to eastern Germany: which on paper emerged as a posting to Stettin as a Corps Commander.

In 1914 the German Army had swept in a vast wheel across Belgium and had reached the River Marne (von Rundstedt, then a Captain, had glimpsed the Eiffel Tower in the distance in September before his unit, along with the rest, had to begin the retreat to the long stalemate in the trenches). Both French and German High Commands had assumed that this attack would happen again, and General Maurice Gamelin had been sure of it when a partly-burnt copy of the German plans was found in the possession of a German major whose plane had made a forced landing in Belgium in January. The plans were still decipherable enough to show the old 'northern wheel'. Gamelin, unwillingly respecting the Low Countries' dogged neutrality, moved his troops up to the Belgian frontier, ready to cross the moment the Germans moved, as he hoped to be able to add Belgium's twenty-two divisions, and perhaps the Dutch ten as well, to his own numbers.

When Jodl reluctantly reported the seizure of the plans to Hitler on 11 January, by which time German troops were moving towards the Low Countries' frontiers, and despite earnest assurances that the remains of the plans showed 'little importance', from that moment the Germans could not feel sure this was so. So on 16 January Hitler ordered the indefinite postponement of Directive Yellow, in order to prepare an entirely new Directive. This proved to be the greatest blessing, giving time to work out a true lightning strike thoroughly. Reports of Allied troop movements showed the strongest Allied units moving to the north, leaving the southern Meuse much more lightly guarded.

Von Manstein was due to leave for Stettin on 9 February. Before that, Army Group A had held manoeuvres, seen by Halder, who was agreeably impressed. He said that Guderian might make an advance of Panzers backed by motorised troops on Sédan. This was a great concession. Hitler's chief military adjutant, Colonel I.G. Schmundt, was present, had a long talk with von Manstein, was much struck by how closely his thoughts resembled Hitler's and were more precisely detailed, and reported back to Hitler, who demanded to see von Manstein at once. Could he not be presented, along with four other newly appointed Corps Commanders, on his way to Stettin? This occurred on 17 February and was a huge success, von Manstein talking all morning, telling Hitler his ideas in detail. Next day Hitler, his work done for him so opportunely, delightedly given what he had wanted all along, called von Brauchitsch and Halder to the Chancellery and gave them the plan as his own work. From that moment all Commanders were united and preparations went forward smoothly and fast. The plan covered everything, and the main thrust was to be Guderian's mighty Panzer spearhead to open the way for Sédan and beyond. This was the core of what came to be known as the Sickle Stroke, one of the most brilliant attack-plans ever devised.

In his enthralling book To Lose A Battle, Alistair Horne gave as a chapter heading for this part of the story Frederick the Great's phrase 'His Majesty, Chance'. Chance had played a part of the highest importance in all this: in the High Command's failure to agree upon a plan, in the break in the weather at the right moment, in the arrival of von Rundstedt and von Manstein at Koblenz, in the professional appreciation von Manstein made, in the amateur intuition of the ex-corporal whose vision left that of his generals far behind, in the loss of the original plans, in the visit of Schmundt to Koblenz, in the timely transfer of von Manstein to Stettin. Napoleon invariably asked about any Commander: 'Has he got luck?' This time indeed a Commander had.

3

Wide is the Gate

The campaign of Holland, Belgium, and France, in which two countries were completely overrun and a third successfully invaded, was a strange example of the way in which the Germans managed to achieve surprise by doing precisely what they had already done twice before.

Philip Guedalla

There was a preliminary to the great Western assault, and that was in Scandinavia, which Hitler had hoped would stay neutral. The Allies' determination to do something helpful there, however, had altered the situation. On 1 March Hitler ordered preparations for an invasion of Norway, using seaborne and parachute troops. The British began their promised mine-laying off the Norwegian coast on 8 April. On the 9th, German forces occupied Denmark, too small to make armed resistance, and captured Oslo, Bergen, Trondhejm and Narvik, as well as every Norwegian airfield they could find.

The Allied Supreme War Council had for some reason decided that if the Allied Expeditionary Force moved towards Norway no aircraft should be sent with it. It was soon dispiritingly clear that air power could, and did, make all the difference. 571 Junkers 52 transport planes carried the six companies of soldiers who rapidly captured Oslo, dropped the 120 paratroops who took Stavanger airfield and enabled 120 Junkers 50 to use it as a base, and (in more than 3,000 sorties) brought into Norway nearly 30,000 men, nearly 260,000 gallons of oil and petrol, and well over 2,000 tons of supplies. In addition came 500 German combat aircraft, three-fifths of them bombers, including at least forty Junkers 87 dive-bombers. These, with their Polish triumphs behind them, introduced untried men of the Allied Services to what was to become one of the most widespread twentieth-century human ordeals. Yet the pattern began to unfold from the first: fear and apprehension, ignorance of how to cope with this new terror, led surprisingly soon to the emergence of qualities to match and then to overcome it, as experience and fortitude did their work.

Even so, this was not to happen for a time. Bomber Command was given two objectives: German shipping off Norway, and the German-occupied airfields. The weather was vile, targets harder than ever to find, and the German fighter pilots knew their job. For example, they shot down six out of twelve Hampdens at Kristiansand on 12 April. 782 sorties against the airfields were made that month at the cost of thirty-one British bombers, but without these doing any very serious damage either. Coastal Command Sunderlands and Hudsons did their best on reconnaissance patrols, but were all too often forced back, if not by German fighters then by the weather. Fighter Command suffered worst. One of their Gladiator squadrons lost all its aircraft in three days, were set up again, then, after sixty-nine combats on three hundred and eighty-nine sorties in twelve days, was reduced to eight. The Hurricane squadron also had twelve days of action, with twenty-six combats on 249 sorties, after which it was down to ten machines. Between them the two squadrons claimed thirty-seven enemy aircraft shot down. By then it was plain that Norway, however reluctantly, must be left to her fate, so the surviving Gladiators and Hurricanes flew off to make their first-ever deck-landings (hitherto thought impossible for them) on the flight deck of the aircraft carrier HMS Glorious. Next day, 9 June, the German battle-cruiser Scharnhorst hit Glorious with her second salvo and she sank within an hour, together with nearly 1500 men of the Royal Navy, forty-one Royal Air Force pilots, and their planes, all invaluable.

The winter had been severe, but uneventful: the spring of 1940 was one of the loveliest in living memory, and was crowded with incident, most of it, from the Allies' point of view, unpleasant.

Only with the opening of the Battle of France did the Royal Air Force, like everyone else, realise exactly what they were up against. The Luftwaffe had until then fought comparatively small-scale actions and the Wehrmacht had not really been fully tested, but both were well prepared and, above all, confident. The French Air Force, weakened by years of changing governments, hesitant policy and reluctance, or inability, to modernise, was further hampered by poor liaison with the French Army, whose High Command did not understand the complete rôle of aircraft in battle. Far too many French politicians had already, deep in their hearts, that corroding doubt about France's ability to win which was to prove fatal. Against all these disadvantages the brave and resolute French airmen could not hope to prevail. On paper the French Army outnumbered the German in men and weapons, and in theory it was absurd to imagine that France might go the way of Poland, but it is a mistake to theorise on the basis of numbers, as many examples in history have mournfully shown. That the German High Command was astonished at its own success, indeed for a time unable to believe it, only underlines the truth of this. What is more to the point for our purpose is that the Royal Air Force, already handicapped by its own country's errors, was now further burdened with the consequences of those of others.

From May 1939 the British authorities had been planning for an Expeditionary Force of thirty-two divisions to be ready for overseas service within a year. Allowing for one squadron per division and one per Army Corps, this meant thirty-nine squadrons. But in addition the Army wanted six for long-range reconnaissance, twenty-four for close-range support, four for liaison, and an unspecified number to cover artillery and transport, which all together might well make a total not far short of a hundred, all working in co-operation with the land forces, just as Coastal Command by its very nature worked with the Royal Navy. This meant that the Royal Air Force would cease to exist as an independent Service. The alarm this reflection caused among Royal Air Force Staff and Commanders alike prompted the creation, in January 1940, of the British Air Force in France Command under Air Marshal Sir Arthur Harris, who, they felt reasonably certain, would be able to reduce the Army's demands to a more realistic level. One added complication, if any were needed, was that both the Advanced Air Striking Force and the Air Component tended to regard their special duties, bombing and reconnaissance, as quite separate, though both were united in deploring the shortage of available fighters. By 10 May there were eight squadrons of Battles and two of Blenheims. There were also two of Hurricanes, joined on that day by a third which was in action within an hour of arrival (it included the young man we shall see later who had danced at the Dorchester the night before). Hurricane No 1 Squadron had profited by the later part of the 'phony war' to observe and imitate the French tactic of having two fighters weaving above and behind every formation, to guard it from being 'jumped'. As until 10 May Belgium had remained neutral, it had not been possible to fly over Belgian territory on reconnaissance, so most of the Blenheims and Lysanders were flung untried into battle. The Hurricanes had not much more experience.

Against them was a formidable force indeed. 1,300 long-range bombers, 380 dive-bombers, 1,210 fighters, 600 reconnaissance aircraft and 475 transport planes, a total of over 4,000 machines, opened the battle, supplying in one day a fresh instalment in the history of air power. The overall German plan was now a masterpiece, concealing its main thrust in the leafy camouflage of the Ardennes by two elaborate flanking schemes, the carefully leaked and unobtrusively emphasised northern invasion of The Netherlands and Belgium which the Allies mistook for the real main attack, and the southern show of strength facing the Maginot Line. Composed as we know of only nineteen divisions, these were of infantry only, and had little to do beyond being there to keep large French forces tied to the huge unwieldly complex of Maginot.

Another historical irony appeared at precisely this time. On Thursday 9 May both British and French Governments came to a changing-point. In Paris the one hundred and ninth Ministry of the Third Republic (averaging well over one a year) resigned. In London, Chamberlain was forced to resign as Prime Minister. So at what may indeed be called the moment of truth, the French leadership was once more in disarray: the British, however, had stepped clear of ambiguities and within twenty-four hours would have found their right leader.

The Luftwaffe took off in strength at Friday's first light, principally covering the Allied ground forces heading full tilt, according to plan, across northern Belgium. Without knowing it until too late, they were presenting the easier target. The Luftwaffe were in the air hours in advance of any Allied aircraft. This had two principal effects. By the end of that momentous Friday the Germans had captured a gratifying number of airfields and bridges in the Low Countries and had destroyed at least half of the small Dutch and much of the almost equally small Belgian air strength, reinforcing their advantage. At the same time the Allies were not giving a thought to the Ardennes. The close-packed Panzer columns approaching there gave the Luftwaffe pilots what one of them called the sight of a lifetime. The Panzer Commanders knew it was also the

38

target of a lifetime, and kept looking apprehensively upwards, only to be always comforted by seeing the familiar black crosses on the wings overhead.

This disastrous day gave the Royal Air Force one slender thread of comfort. The Hurricanes, hardly pausing for breath as it were, flew more than two hundred sorties, claiming forty-two enemy aircraft shot down for the loss of four, and had the great satisfaction of knowing that they could expect a considerable rate of success from their own skill and the quality of their machines. Had they known it, there was something else to be thankful for, though the full benefits would not show just yet. All their senior Commanders had spent their lives in military aviation, steadily winning promotion in training, experience and command. The Luftwaffe Commanders had had shorter, more haphazard careers, always against a background of the politics of violence, and, moreover, as part of the Army structure, with none of the Royal Air Force's refreshing independence. Dowding judged the Luftwaffe as about equal in technical skill and courage, but very different in spirit, which he attributed to the British having had longer to evolve their set-up while the Germans had a quicker and jerkier development. Of course the Luftwaffe had already had battle experience, but he did not think that would prove a vital difference.

It is known that the French Air Force was notably engaged, and bravely too, on 10 May, but its records were lost during the enemy occupation of France or buried fathoms deep in the sombre fastnesses of Vincennes, so there is no way of knowing the exact figures. What is perfectly clear is that the day was a landmark in battle. For the first time the decisive opening stroke of a major European campaign had been provided by the Air, for neither side's armies had so much as caught a glimpse of each other – at any rate in the North.

The Royal Air Force losses on that day were forty-two. At their airfield at Condé-Vraux near Reims the Blenheims of 114 Squadron had just taxied into position for take-off when nine Dorniers came in low, their bombs smashed up the Blenheims and, of course, touched-off their bomb-loads. One Dornier circled while one of its crew took a film before flying away. Eight Battles headed for Belgium and only one, badly damaged, returned. The French High Command, still clinging to its refusal to consider the passage of the Ardennes as practical despite warnings from French airmen who had seen signs of the massive troop-concentrations near Trier, remained blind to the spearhead in the South. Moreover they were still thinking in terms of the 1914 rate of advance. (They were not alone in this: Churchill himself did not realise it for nearly a week.) Guderian, never as we know a man for hanging about, had replied when a senior Commander had said it would take nine days to reach the Meuse that he could do it in four, and he actually arrived there in two. Leaving, like the Luftwaffe, at first light on Friday, he crossed the Luxembourg border at Vianden at half-past five, and reached the Belgian frontier at nine o'clock with hardly a shot fired. The total casualties in Luxembourg were six policemen and a soldier wounded. Seventy-five soldiers were taken prisoner. No one was killed.

In order to prevent the Dutch from resorting to their age-old tactics of repelling invaders by flooding wide areas and destroying bridges, the Germans used paratroops to capture key airfields and take the Maas estuary bridges, though they failed to seize the three Maastricht bridges as the Dutch blew them up as the Panzers were approaching. It was twelve noon before the Germans managed to get an assault-bridge across. They failed similarly at Arnhem and were similarly held up there. But the advance went on. The most vital target in Belgium was the supposedly impregnable great fort at Eben Emael near Liège, and this, in a brilliantly planned coup assiduously rehearsed in complete secrecy for months, was made helpless after a picked force of sappers arrived silently in gliders in the dark, landed on the roof, and pushed explosives down the air-shafts. The eleven-hundred men of the garrison surrendered next day. Twenty-three Belgians had been killed and fifty-nine wounded, six Germans killed and fifteen wounded.

On Whit Sunday 12 May nine Blenheims of 139 Squadron were sent to Maastricht and only one returned, and a following group of twenty-four Blenheims of Bomber Command lost ten. Two of the fifteen Battles of the Belgian Air Force attacking the Albert Canal bridges were shot down. Six volunteer Battle crews from 12 Squadron were called for: every man stepped forward, so the first six crews on the duty roster were accepted. Five took off (the sixth, finding their wireless faulty, changed to another plane only to find the hydraulics out of order) and flew to the bridges. At Vroenhaven only one survivor struggled back, one aircraft was shot down and captured, the other was shot down and destroyed, Flying Officer D.E. Garland and Flight Sergeant T. Gray being posthumously awarded the VC (not given, no one knows why, to their air gunner, Leading Aircraftman L.R. Reynolds). The 'extreme gallantry' of the squadron was noted in the despatches.

This tragic exploit was all the more distressing because the airmen were going after the wrong target. Guderian's force was driving straight for the Meuse. To linger over targets now on the wrong side of Brussels was worse than wasteful. The French Air Force reported accurately, General d'Astier telling Headquarters that 'considerable motorised and armoured forces are approaching the Dinant-Bouillon area' which indicated that 'one can assume a very serious enemy effort'. Headquarters persisted in thinking d'Astier must have got it wrong. Horrified, d'Astier asked the British for help, whereupon fifteen Battles were sent towards Bouillon and six of them failed to return.

What d'Astier's observers had seen was von Rundstedt's Army Group A with seven Panzer divisions as its spearhead, making what was later known to be the most decisive thrust ever yet seen in the history of arms. But what Commanders at French Headquarters, and the overall French Commander Gamelin, had still not realised was that the methods of attack had changed for good and all. That the initial softening-up might be achieved by the air arm had never occurred to them. They knew that much of the German artillery was still horse-drawn, and that to move up the big guns took time, as it always had. They also never imagined it possible that their troops could be thrown into panic by preliminary dive-bombing. Yet this is what happened. The Junkers 87 appeared on the scene like a thunderclap. German troops who watched the assaults and who after all were in no danger from them stood as if turned to stone, hardly able to believe their eyes. As for the recipients, they panicked. Panic is of course highly contagious, so it spread fast to one battery after another. Since the time of the

Master Gunner Napoleon the Artillery had been regarded as France's crack troops, which made their collapse now particularly demoralising. Within hours the first rumours reached Paris and did their damage there: the Stukas became overnight a legend in the annals of terror. This ironically prolonged the life of the Junkers 87 still further, with, as critics bitterly observed later, a very bad effect on the subsequent development of newer German aircraft.

On Whit Monday, Dowding was asked to send thirty-two more Hurricanes, two full squadrons, to France. Still determined to hold on to every possible fighter for England's defence, and by now more certain with every passing hour that it would come to this before long, he asked permission to state his case to the War Cabinet. He took with him a graph he had prepared, laid it before Churchill, and said that, if the present rate of loss went on for another two weeks, there would not be a Hurricane left in France or in this country (emphasising the last four words). Churchill was impressed, but was, as always, torn by his romantic devotion to France, and he stuck to his demands. Dowding therefore prepared a letter to the Under-Secretary of State for Air saying that, while he hoped there might yet be victory in Western Europe, the possibility of defeat must be faced. Defeat in France must surely mean that England would have to fight on alone, so it was essential to keep what he called minimum fighter strength. He asked to be told what that minimum strength should be, so that he could make his plans accordingly. Newall promptly sent copies of the letter to the other Chiefs of Staff and told them bluntly that a few more squadrons could not turn the tide in France, whereas they might make all the difference at home. One vital concession to Dowding resulted from this. Any squadrons now sent to operate in France would be based in England, on airfields close to the south coast. Within days Churchill had come round to the new viewpoint, noting that no matter what French needs were no more squadrons could leave England. During the previous days the ten Hurricane squadrons then in France had lost over half their number.

Dowding's characteristic reaction to the welcome news that no more fighter squadrons were to be based in France was to say that the situation was now *serious* rather than *desperate*. (By the end of May his losses were down to eight a day, while the enemy losses were three or four times that, though he never forgot that Germany had far more aircraft to lose.) The main reason why it was so much better to fight over England than over France was, of course, that shot-down pilots were seldom, or comparatively seldom, killed, and, with no risk of their being taken prisoner, they could quickly be back on operations. The aircraft could usually be repaired too. As we have noticed, he had all along tried to hold on to his Spitfires for home defence, so he was worrying about those which were making sorties across the Channel, some of them several a day. Never for a moment did he lose sight of the importance of the defence of England. He placed it above everything else.

For a day or two before 10 May Peter Parrott and his colleagues at Vitry-en-Artois had been under orders to have three aircraft at readiness half an hour before sunrise, which was at about a quarter to five. Therefore they had to be ready by a quarter past four. Their Mess was in a requisitioned private house in the middle of the village and they were in billets. On the tenth itself, at four in the morning, Parrott and two other pilots were drinking tea in the Mess while they waited for the truck to take them to the airfield. 'We heard the truck arrive and then the clatter of boots on the stone floor as the driver ran in, shouting that there were German aircraft flying overhead.' They dashed out to the truck. At the airfield they grabbed their parachutes and helmets and ran to their planes, which the ground crew had already started up.

> It happened that I was the first away and I started climbing towards two Heinkel 111s flying at about 5,000 feet in a north-easterly direction. There was no sign of any fighter escort for the Heinkels. I was some way below and astern, so had to climb to their height. It was a long chase as I slowly closed the gap. I was still not quite in range when I saw that we were nearing the Belgian frontier. We had had frequent reminders that we must not violate Belgian neutrality and that if we should be forced to land in Belgium we would be interned. So, knowing that I was not close enough to be sure of a hit, I reluctantly opened fire. The gunner of the nearest Heinkel ceased to return fire pretty soon, which was encouraging, but I had to break away at the border. My ammunition ran out at the same time. Only after landing did I learn that the Germans had invaded the Low Countries just a few hours previously. The Heinkels had made a heavy raid on Arras, severely damaging the Headquarters and communication-lines of the British Expeditionary Force.
>
> I flew a further four patrols on that first day, and ten more on the following five days. The other pilots were doing similar intensive flying.

It was customary on these patrols for the twelve Hurricanes to fly in four groups of three, each in a V-formation. One patrol was flying between Louvain and Namur, which was then thought to be part of the front line. Parrott was in the left-hand aircraft of the rearmost V.

> I was one of the first to be hit. Two loud bangs on the armour-plated seat-back was the first intimation I had of the attack, and I took immediate and violent evasive action, descending in a steep spiral. I pulled out of this descent, still turning steeply, and looked round for my assailant, but he was nowhere in sight, nor were any other aircraft, friendly or hostile. Many other pilots had this strange experience of being in the midst of a lot of milling aircraft one moment, and then a few seconds later finding themselves in an empty sky.

This is true. Many pilots had testified to it. It was one of the most uncanny things they vividly remember, looking round and thinking in amazement 'but where have they all gone?'

Parrott returned to Vitry, where he found that:

> The two bangs I had heard were the only two bullets to have hit the aircraft. One had wrecked the radio, and the other had broken a light strut in the fuselage. Repairs were quickly effected.
>
> Reinforcements had arrived from England in the form of sections of three or six aircraft from home-based squadrons, but no extra ground crew, so our own people were hard pressed to service the new aircraft as well as ours and to repair battle damage where it occurred. They worked magnificently.

On 14 May six of us were ordered to Villeneuve, near Épernay, to escort Fairey Battles on a bombing raid. When we arrived the only Battle in sight was one standing on its nose in the middle of the landing area. We were told that the Battles had already gone out on a raid but might fly another in the afternoon. We waited until late in the afternoon, but no Battles returned. So we flew back to Vitry.

Little news, none of it 'hard news' and most of it unreliable, filtered through to Vitry. There were of course plenty of rumours. But one thing was not a rumour, for they all saw it for themselves: the refugees. The road on the east side of the airfield, the road from Lille and Douai, was crowded:

> Cars, farm carts, barrows and bicycles, all piled high with household possessions, passed with what seemed an endless stream of frightened and desperate old men, old women, children and babies. Many asked for help, and our ground crew gave away much of their own rations, and, when they could, they helped with repairs to some of the vehicles.

Hitler had quietly left Berlin late on Thursday night in a special train for his personal command-post in the Eifel and had passed a nervous day and a sleepless night. But when on Saturday morning he heard of the Allied advance into Belgium, proving that his feint in the North had worked, he was transported with joy. The enemy had obligingly fallen into the trap. There was little or nothing to stop the Panzers now.

There was nothing, not even a tiny army's bravery, that could save the Dutch. They had twice Belgium's population but only half the size of Belgium's Army, and by the end of Whit Sunday it had to fall back into 'Fortress Holland', the Amsterdam-Utrecht-Rotterdam area backing on to the sea. Alarmed, the French began withdrawing from the direction of Holland, and Queen Wilhelmina and the Dutch Government made preparations to leave for England next day.

Despite the reports of d'Astier and others who had seen what was coming out of the Ardennes, the French High Command was, even yet, still making air attacks in the North the first priority, with corresponding heavy losses.

German eyes were on Guderian, now drawing near the banks of the Meuse. He had crossed the Semois, and, after narrowly missing being injured by broken glass when a Battle's bomb splintered a window in the Hotel Panorama at Bouillon, in a foray of fifty Battles from which eighteen did not return, he moved his Headquarters three miles north to Noirefontaine. French artillery was bombarding Bouillon, and five French fighters claimed seventeen Stukas shot down.

But Guderian and his men could now see through the sunlit haze the heights of Frénois across the Meuse. It was there, seventy years before, that King Wilhelm I of Prussia, standing with Bismarck to watch the last despairing charge of the French cuirassiers in the Battle of Sédan, had exclaimed in sorrowful admiration: '*Ah, les braves gens!*' Sédan was a magical word to Germans: in 1870 parvenu Prussia had defeated great France there after a neat six-week campaign that united Germany and made Wilhelm the first German Emperor. And here they were again.

43

But something of particular interest was happening further along the Meuse towards Dinant.

Here was the Seventh Panzer Division, with three battalions, 218 tanks in all, most of them Czech-made 'light-mediums'. Their Commanding Officer was a forty-eight year old Major-General who had spent his military life with the Infantry until at his own request he was transferred early in 1940. He arrived to take over the Seventh Panzer at Bad Godesberg on 15 February and rapidly mastered armoured techniques, so much so that his division became the most successful of all. He had a well-earned reputation for quick, daring infiltration and decisive movement, seizing every opportunity and brilliantly making the most of them. His name was Erwin Rommel.

Starting in the early hours of Whit Monday, using rubber boats and a cable-ferry to take guns and groups of men across the river, one hundred and twenty yards wide at that point, while his tanks moved up and down the road firing at the pill-boxes and gun-emplacements on the French side and silencing them one by one, Rommel established tiny bridgeheads. He crossed the Meuse himself several times that day, and, as the French began piecemeal to draw back, began to get his tanks across on pontoons. He only did it by a hair's breadth: a resolute counter-attack would have stopped him, and until morning on 14 May his position was dangerous in the extreme. His personal leadership was masterly, he was 'everywhere at once'.

Guderian's Panzers were massing in the riverside valleys opposite Sédan. His infantry was now beginning to come into the picture, healthy sun-tanned shirt-sleeved young men with the sun in their eyes striding up through the tall grass and spring flowers. They could see beyond Sédan the great height of La Marfée, from which the French General Grandsard could see them, thinking longingly 'What a target!' – yet limiting his guns to thirty to eighty rounds each. He remarked that there was plenty of time, the enemy would be unable to get his guns up for several days. Grandsard had forgotten the Luftwaffe.

But not for long. They appeared at seven o'clock in the morning on Monday, aiming particularly at the communication-lines, and going on until at noon the sky was full of aircraft, wave after wave, the Stukas peeling off for their dives three at a time, while the rest watched and then followed up. Guderian had worried lest they might have been ordered to make a single mass attack, and said as much to Lieutenant-General Bruno Loerzer, who replied that 'Yes, such an order had come in, but, well, let's say, too late'. French casualties were not heavy, but the effect was: Grandsard's troops were not hardened, and their morale broke.

The French Air Force had not been called in, General Billotte having said something about 'two or three days' which showed that he too was estimating the rate of advance far too slowly, and the French Commander near Givonne saying that bombers were not required as the artillery were firing. The Royal Air Force spent much of the day patching itself up, as well it might, for its losses in three days had been appalling. Four-tenths lost on the 10th, all sorties on the 11th, two-thirds on the 12th, by the end of which its 135 operational bombers had fallen to seventy-two. Sir Arthur Barratt had received a message from the Air Staff in London saying that this rate of loss could not go on: 'If we expend all our efforts in the early stages of the battle we shall not be able to operate effectively when the really critical stage comes'. London did not realise that the critical stage was now, this minute.

Monday 13 May, as the day when the first Germans forced the passage of the Meuse, was the most decisive single move made in any campaign. It was not clear at the time, though it became clear very soon, that this day was the Allies' last chance. If they could not seriously damage and delay the German spearhead then, they could not do it at all. The Luftwaffe, whose day this was, cut road and rail supply-lines, preventing command-posts from knowing what was going on elsewhere and stopping orders from getting through, creating as much chaos as possible. The Luftwaffe was operating under almost copy-book conditions. This is illustrated by Guderian's first order on the morning of 14 May: 'The divisions will capture their objectives according to the map exercise'.

Tuesday the 14th looked at first as though it were going to be more satisfying for the Royal Air Force, as they began to carry out a series of bomb-attacks. 103 and 150 Squadrons made ten early sorties with no loss except for one forced landing. But then the French called for attacks on the Germans at Sédan. The French Air Force attacked first with severe losses. Between three and four in the afternoon seventy-one AASF bombers took off escorted by a large force of fighters. This represented the entire bomber strength in France. German fighters appeared in strength. But Guderian, who had foreseen all kinds of attacks and had dealt with the subject in his *Achtung – Panzer!*, had detached his flak batteries from his main force and quickly brought them up to the pontoon bridge sites. The kind of fire-power which would have stopped the Stukas if the Allies had possessed it was therefore waiting for the Battles and Blenheims when they arrived, and for the Hurricanes which joined them. At the trifling cost to the Germans of some damage to two or three of the pontoon bridges the Royal Air Force lost seventy-one aircraft, forty bombers and thirty-one fighters – one watching German counted eleven in less than an hour from the point were he stood. Its experiences on that day were compared by Alistair Horne with Tennyson's Valley of Death ('Then they rode back, but not, Not the six hundred . . . Back from the mouth of Hell'). Many Germans praised their 'incredible bravery'. The 56 per cent loss suffered by the bombers on this day was the highest loss rate ever suffered by RAF bombers. Bomber Command's losses on raids into Germany later in the war rarely exceeded 10 per cent in each raid. The Battles were only once to attack again in strength during the Battle of France, when thirty-eight aircraft attacked German positions on the Marne on 13 June; six aircraft were lost to 88mm flak.

That Tuesday, 14 May, the Germans' business was to establish securely their bridgeheads on the Meuse. The Tenth Panzer broke across on the southern side of Sédan and, gaining the heights of Thélonne, found the French artillery positions deserted, guns still standing loaded. Along with the motorcycle units, their job was now to hold the high ground at Stonne, commanding the Sédan area from the south. The First and Second Panzers crossed north of Sédan, where Guderian was able to grasp the weakness of the whole French position. At that moment he decided to wheel his force to the right, cross the Ardennes Canal which would allow him to cut between the French Second and Ninth Armies, come out on to the north-eastern plain and head for the coast. His order was given in seven words: 'For the right wheel, road map Rethel'. He paused for a moment above Donchéry, looking back at the ground his men had come over: 'The success of our attack struck me as almost a miracle'.

That same morning, negotiations for a cease-fire in Holland began. The Luftwaffe planned to bomb Rotterdam as an act of terror, to convince the Dutch that they had no hope, though their readiness to discuss a cease-fire shows that they had realised this themselves. At two in the afternoon the bombing-raid took place against the ancient centre of the undefended city, a twenty-minute assault by sixty Heinkel 111s. That was The Netherlands' last straw, and Rotterdam joined Guernica, Madrid, Barcelona and Warsaw, images of cities shattered and burning, whose names produce a frisson in the mind. The Dutch Foreign Minister said that 30,000 people had been killed in less than ten minutes, and though it was later established that the true figure was 980, which is quite bad enough, the 'thirty thousand' is still quoted. 20,000 buildings were destroyed, 15,000 people made homeless, and over a square mile of the city was in flames. At this point the Dutch surrendered, concluding the instrument of surrender next day.

At half-past seven on Wednesday morning Churchill woke up to find the French Prime Minister Paul Reynaud on the telephone, telling him: 'We have been defeated, we have lost the battle'. Churchill's natural reaction was: 'So soon?' He realised then just how utterly matters had changed since 1918, that now in 1940 a full advance of fast and heavy armour with a strong air force could do in a few days what in the previous war had taken years to accomplish. At eleven o'clock, just as the Dutch were completing their surrender, the War Cabinet met in London. Item Two on the agenda had two points to discuss, whether more fighter squadrons should be sent to France, and whether or not to bomb the Ruhr. It may seem strange that just then, when the crisis had come in France, the main preoccupations regarding the Royal Air Force should have been centred upon Britain (fighters) and Germany (bombers). The answer to the first question was No, the second Yes. When the welcome news about his fighters reached Dowding, he called it a notable victory, but added with his customary clear insight that there were sure to be more appeals from France and it remained to be seen how the Cabinet's decision would stand the test of time. That part of the discussion had taken far less time than did the bomber question. Among those in favour was the Lord Privy Seal, Clement Attlee, who said it was essential now to make a counter-attack of some kind. Quite a number of people said that bombing the Ruhr might well deflect some of the German forces to the defence of the Ruhr. The final decision gave undisguised pleasure to the Royal Air Force representatives present. The first attack was ordered as soon as possible.

Air Marshal Sir Arthur Barratt, who after all was in France and therefore knew a lot more about what was really happening, decided that day that French-based bombers must not henceforth be used in daylight except in grave emergency, which left only the English-based Bomber Command Group Two, and thirty-eight French bombers, to operate during the day. By mid-day he heard that half the French fighter force of 237 was now unserviceable, some of them on their own airfields.

Both the Cabinet decisions worried one man, the Commander of the British

Air Marshal Sir Arthur Barratt, CB, CMG, MC, at his desk at HQ in France.

Expeditionary Force. Lord Gort was stationed east of Brussels, and, though aware that there was a good deal of action on and near the Meuse, knew little else about it. What he did know was that his own forces expected to be fully engaged very soon, and would need all the fighter cover they could get. They would also require bombers to attack the German supply-lines and communications as the Luftwaffe had already done with the French. He wondered what good it would do to bomb the Ruhr if the Battle of France was going to be lost. Such Hurricanes as were available were operating magnificently, but there was nothing like enough of them, and they were being showered with calls for help, from the Belgians, from the French, from other Royal Air Force units – far more calls than they could possibly meet. Gort and his senior officers fervently wished that Dowding would release his Spitfire squadrons, but, as we know, he was hoarding them like gold, for he knew how much they would be needed later.

Meanwhile a mixed force of bombers, Whitleys, Hampdens and Wellingtons, made ready to bomb the Ruhr. No one seems to know the exact number: accounts vary from ninety-six to a hundred and five. Oil-plants were the main target, marshalling-yards the secondary target. Only a third of the attacking aircraft claimed to have reached their objectives. One Wellington was lost. Even the most optimistic could not call this a strong blow at the enemy, but the Air Staff seemed to think it quite a satisfactory start, saying that the oil-plants might possibly be destroyed in the next few days if the whole bombing effort were made against them (author's italics). For the rest of the month 430 bombing sorties were launched on eleven nights with 535 tons of bombs, and the result was that German supply and production went serenely on, while not a single German plane was withdrawn from France. It has been pointed out by more than one commentator that Germany did not see her actions in terms of damage or casualties, but judged everything in the light of the objectives she was aiming for: and she was aiming, very confidently indeed, for victory in France, and at top speed too. With hindsight we can see that, while the fighter decision was right, the bomber decision was wrong, but this was not apparent for a time.

During the Battle of France, replacement Hurricanes were flown across the Channel by Royal Air Force ferry-pilots. These pilots were told to hand over the Hurricanes and return at once to England in transport planes. There were, however, occasions when necessity on the spot abruptly altered these arrangements, when losses among pilots as well as machines forced hard-pressed squadron commanders to take over both. With remarks like 'You may think you're going back to England, chum, but you've had it – use that Hurricane yourself and we'll find you a billet for the night', the ferry-pilots sometimes found themselves hurled into battle. It was all too easy for the names of these hurriedly conscripted men not to be entered on the squadron papers, which could, and did, cause no end of confusion if one of them had the ill-luck to be posted as missing.

Flying Officer Richard Gayner, old Etonian, later to become a Lloyd's underwriter, commenting on or about 20 May, said that his unit had lost a third of its aircraft and pilots already. It was exhausting to go on getting up at first light and then making several sorties a day, every day. The Luftwaffe had such vast numbers – the sky seemed full of them, especially the Messerschmidt 109s – and were so well equipped, while the Royal Air Force had the additional handicap of receiving very few communications from Headquarters or from their Wing, for the Germans pounded anything resembling communications or military buildings. Small wonder they were better at their job than the British were just then, he thought. Flight Lieutenant R D G Wight's opinion was similar but had a more hopeful feeling: the best the British could do was fifty times better than the best the Germans could do, machine for machine, pilot for pilot, but the advantage at the moment lay with the larger forces. Wight knew of no Royal Air Force pilot who had flinched from combat whatever the odds, and sometimes the odds were fifty to one. He and two other pilots were on one occasion almost out of ammunition and dangerously low on petrol when they saw a dozen Junkers 88s escorted by over eighty Messerschmidt 109s. The three British men went straight in and, as Wight put it, the enemy finally left the Hurricanes alone. One sergeant shot down three fighters and a bomber before he in turn was shot down, and he contrived to get back to England in a rescuing ship. Wight made no bones about it: if, he said, there was only one British pilot and one British aircraft left against the whole of the Luftwaffe, that pilot would take that plane into action against them. (Wight practised what he preached: he was killed two months later leading his Section of Hurricanes into battle against sixty Messerschmidt 110s.)

Flying Officer Christopher Foxley-Norris went to France with an Army Co-operation squadron of Lysanders and, as he said, lost twelve out of twelve, the lot. Those who were neither rescued nor dead after baling-out had to make their way back to the coast as best they could, sheltering among clumps of trees or in forests, sleeping rough, taking particular precautions when getting food or approaching any local inhabitants. There were dispiriting stories, too many to be lightly dismissed, of French people only too ready to betray their presence to the enemy. Pilot Officer Patrick Hancock, near St Nazaire and preparing with his companions to get away from France, was told perfectly seriously by the French colonel in charge of the airfield ground defences that they should surrender to him, to be handed over to the Germans when (author's italics) Paris fell.

Flying Officer Barrie Heath, later to become Chairman of GKN Ltd, experienced his baptism of fire when his Section dived down upon a large formation of Stukas. He shot one up, which so excited him that he went on firing until he had no ammunition left. There seemed, he thought, no point in hanging about after that, so, as he put it, he beetled off home. – And did not allow himself to get quite so excited in his subsequent sorties.

A more complicated exploit was commented upon by Squadron Leader James Leathart. He was commanding 54 (Spitfire) Squadron based at Hornchurch along with 74 Squadron whose commander was Squadron Leader Drogo White. Leathart saw a Spitfire shot down at Calais Marck, and on landing back at Hornchurch was told that White was missing. Certain that it was he who had gone down at Calais, Leathart asked if he could go back in a Miles Master training plane to fetch White out, and if his two Flight Commanders could escort him in their Spitfires. The Station Commander ('Master' in RAF slang) gave permission, and off they went, landing correctly at Calais Marck, where they saw no sign of White. The three aircraft took off to cruise about, but they were barely airborne when some Messerschmidts appeared. The two Spitfires gave chase at once, while Leathart, considerably startled, re-landed and, hearing the rattle of machine-guns overhead, took refuge in a ditch where another airman was prudently hiding. Incredibly this man was White, and they greeted each other with relief. How in the world, Leathart wondered, did the Germans not suspect anything strange about the bright orange aircraft he had arrived in? The heartening fact remains that they ignored it. At the same time there were German tanks and motor-cycles roaring past on the road skirting the airfield perimeter. After a while the noise of traffic quietened down and the two pilots thought it was time to go. Now came another problem. The Miles Master had no electric starter, as it invariably had at Hornchurch, so the engine had to be cranked-up like an old-fashioned motor-car. After what seemed like hours of cranking (with more German transport still passing along the road), the engine started, the two pilots jumped in, and flew thankfully away, crossing the Channel, with the wheels still down, just a few feet clear of the water throughout the journey. Leathart, who had never flown a Master before, was awarded the DSO for the reserve.

Flying Officer Peter Matthews had a simpler departure from France, but an untidy one. The idea was, of course, to get every serviceable aircraft away. There were a few

Czechs and Poles at the airfield, and they said they could fly, so they were told to take a plane each and fly north, hoping that they would manage to land in England. The same thing happened to the squadron's French interpreter, who was put into a plane and flew it back safely. Then the rest of the squadron departed. It is fascinating to find this kind of comment, which, like most of these reports, clearly reflects the readiness to improvise and take chances, to do the best one can with the materials to hand, never mind how, never mind in what order, so long as it is done. The contrast between all these cheerful makeshifts and the careful, prudent, systematic attitude of officials who, come what may, stick to the regulation procedures at all costs, is always piquant. And it is a contrast that can be found whenever both groups, those in action and those in the office, are engaged together, as in war. It is worth remembering that both are needed. Without the system in existence, everything falls to pieces. Without the willingness to take risks and quick decisions on the spot, victory is not attainable.

A flight of Hurricanes leaving an aerodrome 'somewhere in England' for patrol over France.

Two at least of the Hurricane pilots started the War in unusual ways. One had been on leave, and on 9 May went to a dance at the Dorchester, cheerfully going to bed at his club at three in the morning. At eight a manservant woke him with tea and the news of the German invasion. The pilot wasted no time. After making ready as quickly as possible he drove at speed to Tangmere where he arrived at half-past eleven. He was told that 501 Squadron would take off for France at one o'clock. At four o'clock he was ordered to fly off on reconnaissance. The smoke of battle was visible ahead of him when he suddenly noticed a pack of Messerschmidt 109s bearing down on him, whereupon he dived his Hurricane at full throttle, not daring, he said afterwards, to glance at his Air Speed Indicator. The Messerschmidts were firing at him but he straightened out, dangerously close to the tree-tops, managed to dodge, and landed back safely at his French airfield. What with one thing and another, it had been quite a day.

The other pilot started very well on 11 May by shooting down two bombers, but the German flak got him before he could turn away and he crash-landed in a field. There were German tanks and soldiers near by, but the Hurricane was out of sight of them, all they could see was a man in an overcoat. They assumed he was a local refugee and locked him up in a barn for the time being. The barn had a window and outside the window was a ladder. The pilot got out, made his way back somehow (he could put it no clearer than that), and was flying again next day.

Combat reports giving details of escapes are comparatively rare: if the aircraft was a Defiant, even rarer. Pilot Officer McLeod was flying his Defiant, along with four others, near Rotterdam when they saw four Junkers 87 dive-bombers attacking ground targets near a railway. The Defiants went in to attack. McLeod's air gunner shot one down in flames, at which moment a Messerschmidt came up behind him. After a brisk exchange of fire, the air gunner reported all four of his guns out of action, and, while he was re-cocking them, McLeod side-slipped and manoeuvred, going towards another Defiant which was being chased by two 109s. Another 109 appeared on Mr McLeod's tail.

> I carried out the same action as before but turned so quickly that I had to encounter with a high speed stall and a spin, and when coming out I noticed both starboard and port petrol tanks on fire, the gunner also told me that the guns were finally out of action, perhaps due to lack of ammunition, he could not say.

There was nothing for it but to make a forced landing. Just as the two men scrambled out safely, the Defiant went up in flames.

The entire area seemed to be occupied by the German Army, but fortunately the two were inconspicuous in their covering overalls and nondescript civilian overcoats. They took shelter in a Dutch house nearby where they hid under the cellar stairs. A German armoured car stopped outside and the soldiers searched the house, but failed to find them, though the Germans stayed in the house for over three hours. Soon after they finally left, McLeod and his companion slipped out and lay low in a ditch a couple of hundred yards away. 'From then on it was a case of hide and seek until we came to a river.' The air gunner could not swim, so the two men walked along the bank towards a bridge. This turned out to be guarded by Germans who shouted at them, but they pretended not to hear, sat on the bank and were thenceforth ignored, even when after an hour or so they rose to their feet and strolled away in the opposite direction. When they saw a house on the far bank they watched it to see whether it was enemy-occupied,

> but it did not seem to be, so we whistled across to the occupants who rowed us over and gave us the direction of the Dutch Regiment (Sixth Infantry) who were about six kilometres away.

On the way to find the Regiment they saw plenty of air activity – Heinkel 111s making bombing-raids, Messerschmidt 109s guarding them and more 109s flying in loose, ever-shifting formation towards the coast. They identified themselves to the Dutch Sixth Infantry and discovered several things: the Dutch Commanding Officer was panic-stricken and seemed to have no idea what to do, his men were good types but over-ready, in McLeod's opinion, to argue with their officers, and the Regiment was preparing to retreat to Antwerp that night to avoid being surrounded. The two Britons decided to go on alone, but in the end were driven to Antwerp in one of the lorries. At Antwerp the British Consul-General engaged French soldiers to take them on to Ghent, where the British Vice-Consul took them himself to Ostend and got them a passage on the *Prince Leopold* for Folkestone. That night, waiting to sail, the *Prince Leopold* was attacked by bombers which did just enough damage for her passengers to be transferred on to a British ferry, while the two airmen were taken on board the escorting British destroyer, both vessels crossing safely to Dover next day.

McLeod noted in his report that the civilians in the Low Countries had seemed badly demoralised and that the Germans appeared to make little distinction between military and civil objectives to attack.

A note from No 1 (Hurricane) Squadron mentioned crowds of Dorniers passing overhead at regular intervals so that the pilots were told to take everything that could fly into the air and circle like mad round the airfield. One Hurricane doing this had no guns. Another note, from 73 Squadron, called 10 May a day too crammed with incident for any report to do justice to it.

Official Air Ministry papers and reports of the first three days concentrated on what was happening in the Low Countries: no more than the French did they realise what was happening in the Ardennes. The reports carefully account for all actions they knew of, but the whole tone of them is distressingly hopeful, implying that these actions were really managing to check or delay the Germans somehow, somewhere. The unfolding German advance made it clear that resistance was rather like working with pea-shooters against a brick wall. The Allied Commanders, viewed of course with hindsight, resemble a householder with leaky pipes dashing from one to another in vain attempts to plug a gap here or there before the flood breaks through in an unsuspected place. It was 12 May before any mention of the Ardennes was made, when the German advance there was seen to be 'assuming increasingly serious proportions'. It is true that the Germans themselves had deliberately played this down to create the best possible conditions of advance and surprise, stressing in their broadcast reports the activity in the North. It is also true that reports of activity towards and on the Meuse had reached French Headquarters, but these were still not being taken seriously. The truth would come home to them fully only on 15 May – and even then they did not guess right as to just where Guderian was making for.

As far as the rank and file of the Allied forces were concerned, it cannot be too strongly emphasised that the men doing the actual fighting had, as the Royal Air Force put it, not a clue about what was going on anywhere else. 'We were there getting shot at, that's all we knew'. 'No idea what was happening except where we were'. 'Lots of news, some wrong and some right, was broadcast at home long before we heard any of it'.

One news item of great importance was broadcast on 14 May: the appointment of Lord Beaverbrook as Minister of Aircraft Production. Within a month the figures for new fighter aircraft would have trebled: for example, the Februrary total had been 141 but the May figure was going to be 325 and the June figure 446. Not all these aircraft were brand-new. 'The Beaver' set up the Civilian Repair Organisation, whose job it was to restore damaged aircraft to good-as-new condition, and they did this to such effect that in the Battle of Britain itself thirty-five per cent of the fighters were reconditioned ones. Of course, many had been too badly damaged to repair. These, along with enemy write-offs, were taken by the salvage people and their metal melted down to be used afresh.

Lord Beaverbrook's methods were decided, prompt, and ruthless. From the first he ignored what Ministry staffs called proper channels, and, more often than not, by-passed the officials, sending his own men direct to factories and warehouses all over the country. This abrupt change from all that government officers had been used to not merely shook their habitual composure to its foundations but provoked them into agonised clucks of protest, of which he took not the slightest notice. The men he sent out were told to discover exactly what resources, stocks and supplies existed in the country and report these to him. Then they were to go to every airfield they could find and make certain that one of two things happened to damaged aircraft: either each must be repaired, or must be seized to provide spare parts and, when reduced to scrap metal, delivered to the nearest scrap-yard where it could do some good in aircraft-building. He also appealed for anything made of aluminium that anyone could spare, using the catchy slogan 'saucepans into Spitfires'.

Finding that some maintenance units actually still had the mad idea that they could continue closing for the weekend, The Beaver stopped that at once. From now on they would work round the clock, twenty-four hours a day, seven days a week. He reinforced this by a broadcast, emphasising that we had only ourselves to rely on, that our pilots and air gunners were waiting for more aircraft in order to beat the enemy, and we must not let them down. These measures had their effect. Within a few days, aircraft production was up by almost two-thirds.

The warehouses and depots were found to be full of supplies, so he observed that storekeepers think a full store is a good store. On the contrary: they are stagnant. So he sent his people round again, to commandeer everything usable, which must quickly be replaced and delivered. It was tough at first, but then began to work. Cartoons showed The Beaver as a pirate king leading his pirate crew, and he was said to work a seventeen-hour day. Dowding praised him, so did Churchill, and the squadrons were, of course, delighted.

A flight of Battle bombers on reconnaissance near the lines in France.

During 15 May, what had the day before been three small separate bulges of bridgeheads on the Meuse was now a continuous front sixty-two miles wide. No wonder that French historians say that this was really the day on which France lost the War. But who could be expected to realise that then?

Rommel, with all the impetuous dash that was to rouse British admiration in North Africa later, shook himself free of the Meuse, had a brush with the French First Armoured, leaving the following Fifth Panzer to mop up, and pushed on to Philippeville and then to Cerfontaine. This move ensured that Guderian had nothing to worry about on his right flank. Rommel's men were longing for some sleep, they were dirty and unshaven and 'looked like pigs' as one of them said, but by that night Rommel had advanced seventeen miles, taken over four hundred prisoners, put seventy-five French tanks out of action and made the French Ninth Army incapable of counter-attack. He had lost fifteen men killed.

General Reinhardt's Sixth and Eighth Panzers crossed the Meuse at Monthermé and got on the move too. They were astounded to find crowds of French soldiers surrendering without a struggle. Shops were closed in the villages and small towns, houses empty, streets uncannily quiet. A German war diarist could not get over it: he kept thinking of Poland, where hopelessly outnumbered, outgunned and out-manoeuvred Poles had fought bravely on to the end. They and their small country had

54

not been demoralised: why then had France? 20,000 surrendering at one place on one day: why? how? He was not the only man asking that.

But now the whole Panzer force, with the great plain of north-east France stretching before them, could roar on unhindered over clear roads. They did so in the highest spirits. When they needed petrol they stopped at the nearest pumps, filled up, and drove on without paying — as a rule there was no one there to pay anyhow. When they wanted a drink they stopped to milk the nearest cow. They milked the cows any way, having been told to do so as so many of the poor beasts had not been milked and were bellowing for relief. The whole thing seemed almost like a day out, not like part of a full-scale war.

It was less than a week since all this had started. Who could have believed that a war can be lost in six days?

4

Nine Days' Wonder

*Vast black shadows on the pale sands . . . enormous formations of men, standing,
waiting . . . They did not seem to change; they did not seem to sit, nor to lie down;
they stood, with the patience of their race, waiting their turn.*

John Masefield

The French Government was now certain that the Germans were heading for Paris.
Pieces of news reaching Gamelin at Vincennes – the first 'hard' news telephoned direct
from various Commanders in the field – told of Panzers approaching Laon only eighty-
two miles from the capital, of French failure to dislodge the Germans at Stonne, of
the Germans' passing Montcornet, of French withdrawals in disorder, of 20,000
French soldiers having retreated as far as Compiègne. With the usual speed of Parisian
rumour, it was not long before the dread words 'they'll be in Paris by tonight' began
to circulate in the city, helped no doubt by seeing, in the Place de la Concorde, the
staff of the Ministry of Marine hurriedly loading stacks of files on Navy lorries. One
feature of these days, strange to British observers, was the lightning-swift proliferation
of two ominous expressions: 'Who has betrayed us?' and 'Fifth Column'. The first of
these had been heard everywhere in 1870, and in periods of reversal in 1914–1918;
it appears to be the basic French reaction to evil tidings in war, now taking a more
pervasive form than ever in a country where for years contrasted fears had rent French
society. Fears on the one hand of prosperous citizens' right-wing sympathies, on the
other of workers' revolution. Many a time in those terrible weeks people in all walks
of life voiced them with infinitely more abhorrence than they spoke of the foreign
invader. 'Better Hitler than Blum' was often heard, even murmurs of the ancient word
of terror, 'Barricades'. Motor-cars loaded with family belongings began to leave the
French capital, heading south and west. One distinguished foreign journalist met the
sceptical side of the coin, when he remarked soberly to a French scientist: 'They are
in Sédan' and was told he must be dreaming: 'I never knew you were such a
scaremonger' – only to be faced with the midday headline *Sédan evacuated* in the street
outside.

Churchill crossed to France that afternoon. At the Quai d'Orsay he found tragic-faced
French ministers, Gamelin saying that there were no reserves to fall back on,
wheelbarrow-loads of documents burning on bonfires in the garden, and, worst of
all, every Frenchman present, military and civilian, showing clearly his conviction that

France was beaten. To a war-dog like Churchill this was an unimaginable reaction: he talked vigorously, bracingly, telling them how a huge city could absorb whole armies if it were fought through house by house, and managed to kindle a responsive spark in Reynaud's eye: but in no one else's. At nine o'clock that evening he sent the War Cabinet a telegram referring to what he called the mortal gravity of the hour, adding that he felt sure all available British aircraft should be sent at once to give the French Army a chance to rally. This was Churchill the chivalrously romantic devotee of France speaking: subsequent thought, coloured by fuller realisation, brought cooler counsel. He admitted freely that his years in the political wilderness, cut off from state documents, had not enabled him to realise the fundamental changes brought about in warfare by fast, heavy armour (and he had been in office for less than a week). On his way home he and his colleagues agreed that, barring a miracle, the French as a fighting force were done for.

The War Cabinet, after earlier discussion, had rather thought that the equivalent of four more squadrons should be sent to France. Now they toyed with the idea of sending Bomber Command into the battle and ordering the last six Hurricane squadrons in England to fly over from Kent and back each day, three in the morning and three in the afternoon. (The seventh squadron had left for Narvik, where Allied troops were still clinging to their tiny Norwegian toehold.) It was then that Newall provided the Cabinet with copies of Dowding's letter, which made those present vacillate yet again.

Barratt had rung up Newall earlier, reporting that his fighter pilots were very tired after a day of four or five sorties each, in little groups of three or four, against waves of forty enemy bombers with fighter escort. This helped to make Newall realise that Royal Air Force assistance just then was really a drop in the ocean. But before any aircraft could be deployed, events overtook them, for by the end of the following day the Advanced Air Striking Force was under orders to leave France and the Air Component had been told to be ready to follow at half an hour's notice.

If anyone needed more proof, it came from Bomber Command. At ten to five on the morning of the 16th, the day Churchill went to Paris, twelve Blenheims of 82 Squadron took off to block the Germans at Gembloux, north of Namur, where they would rendezvous with Hurricanes. Eleven were shot down before reaching Gembloux. Until then the Air Staff had favoured the use of fighters to 'clear the air' ahead of the bombers. After this catastrophe they realised their mistake. Churchill, probably influenced more than anything else by Newall's blunt 'it would be criminal to compromise the air defence of Great Britain any further', issued his order that no more fighter squadrons were to leave Britain whatever the need in France.

It might be as well to reflect upon Fighter Command's medley of responsibilities and duties at this time. They had to beat off enemy bombers and reconnaissance aircraft over Allied troops, escort and defend Allied bombers in daylight, play their part in daylight fighting, report troop movements. They had to provide cover for the Channel Ports and for Channel convoys, including supply-ships for the Army, and deliver important secret documents to various Army Headquarters. There were distinguished officers and statesmen who had to be safely escorted across the Channel and back. (When Churchill went to France it was in an unarmed Flamingo with a fighter escort.)

All these tasks were signalled urgently and at short notice. And yet all the time the need to build up Fighter Command's strength and increase it was vital.

A measure of the Royal Air Force's hard-pressed activities is shown by Maxwell who, staying at North Weald with his squadron's A Flight, reported B Flight's actions on 17 May. They had flown over the day before to their airfield at Vitry-en-Artois, and made their first patrol at five in the morning. Anti-aircraft fire slightly damaged two Hurricanes. Four Hurricanes took off at eight, returning safely at twenty-past nine claiming a Junkers 88 and a Dornier 17 shot down. Five went on the noon patrol, where, ten miles east of Cambrai, they met ten Heinkel 111s, shot down five and damaged two more. They were then 'jumped' by a formation of Messerschmidt 109s, whereupon four of them dived into cloud and got away; the fifth, piloted by Flight Lieutenant Ian Soden, shot down one Messerschmidt before he too dived away. In mid-afternoon a Dornier dropped a bomb on the airfield, doing negligible damage, and two Hurricanes instantly flew off in pursuit and shot it down.

Next morning they patrolled the Brussels-Ghent area and bagged another Dornier. In the afternoon, three Hurricanes were just taking off when they were attacked by Messerschmidts which damaged one whose pilot got back with difficulty, and shot down the other two, killing both pilots. At seven o'clock that evening Soden shot down one of three Heinkels while other Hurricanes engaged a Messerschmidt 110 which, nicknamed The Destroyer, was itself destroyed. Later, Dorniers again attacked the Vitry airfield and caught Soden just as he was taking off. In his two days of fighting he had accounted for six enemy aircraft, and for his courage in staying to make sure of a kill the day before he was posthumously awarded the DSO.

Harry Broadhurst crossed the path of these Hurricanes at Vitry. He was rung up from Fighter Command and asked if he would like to go to France to command a Fighter Wing.

> I readily agreed, since commanding a Fighter Station with no aeroplanes on it was not my idea of excitement.

He was sent for by his Chief, Air Vice-Marshal Leigh-Mallory, whom he had never seen until then:

> He spent quite a long time trying to persuade me to change my mind. He emphasised that the war in France would only last a few weeks and that then I would find myself in the front line for what was to become the Battle of Britain. I argued that I would prefer to take a chance on that, which seemed to annoy him.

Next day, 18 May, Broadhurst was flown over to France and landed at Amiens in the middle of a bombing-raid. He called this sardonically 'an encouraging start', but he was soon on his way by road to Vitry to command Sixty Wing,

> which was shot up within minutes of my arrival. I found that my predecessor had been invalided home with a nervous breakdown and that the three squadrons on the station were without serviceable squadron commanders. To say that chaos reigned

would be an understatement, and I was soon under orders to retreat with the remains of the Wing to Merville, where I was soon joined by the remnants of another Wing. Normal operations were impossible since the airfield was being attacked day and night, and landing and taking-off were adventures in themselves. The surrounding population was in full retreat and normal amenities such as telephones had virtually ceased to exist.

Within a very short time he was ordered to evacuate the Wings back to England. Most of the men were to be convoyed to Boulogne,

and I was to keep a skeleton ground staff to enable my aircraft to continue operating until six o'clock in the evening when several transport aircraft would arrive to evacuate the remaining ground crew. My aircraft would take off and circle overhead to protect the transports and then escort them back to England.

Broadhurst had left his Hurricane 'ticking-over in the corner of the airfield' while he supervised the loading-up.

I then took off in the Hurricane, but, en route to overhaul the Fighter Escort, I was caught by four Messerschmidt 110s, which damaged the Hurricane somewhat, but I managed to escape, get back to England and land safely.

Whereupon he was 'most surprised' to be told to report immediately to the Commander-in-Chief, Dowding himself.

He wanted an account of my experiences in France. He emphasised that when the Germans reached the French coast, Fighter Command would be subjected to the same sort of war we had experienced in France. He therefore instructed me to tour the Fighter Squadrons in England, and tell them about the sort of battle they could expect, and report back to him in a week's time.

On my last day in France I had organised dumps to be made round the airfield, of equipment which I knew to be in very short supply in Fighter Command. I had hoped to load it on to the transports, but they were already overloaded with just the men. The C-in-C made no comment when I told him, but I later found out that he had sent the transports back with a fighter escort, back to France, where they loaded up all the equipment and brought it safely back to England.

At the same time, Dowding suggested to Newall that it might be helpful for Bomber Command to concentrate not on targets like crossroads and railways which could be repaired quickly, but rather on things which if damaged would positively slow the enemy up, airfields, grounded aircraft, fuel dumps. He also asked, no doubt in the spirit of trying all means of persuasion, for his own commitments to be as limited as possible – unless, if France were defeated, the Government in London intended to surrender: a bold comment at the time and one which he described disarmingly years later as 'rather cheeky'.

By 21 May the only fighters still left across the Channel were what were left of 1, 73 and 501 Squadrons. Maxwell saw some of the pilots coming back to North Weald, tired, grubby and unshaven, and loaded with bottles, some of them bottles of champagne. He asked one pilot if it had been thrilling out there. 'No', said the pilot heavily, 'no, sheer hell, terror from start to finish.'

By then, Reynaud had replaced Gamelin. Reynaud was still in a fighting mood and he wanted a fighting general: General Maxime Weygand, then seventy-three and serving as military commander in Syria. He was a devotee of Foch and was supposed to have imbibed Foch's secrets of successful warfare. He took over on 20 May, and within four days had come round to believing that there was nothing for it, France was going to have to ask for an armistice. But first there must be one last great battle, to save the nation's honour. Weygand had grown up in the shadow of 1870, and of the dread Commune, and he was more nervous of another French revolution, apparently, than of a German occupation. Gamelin, who was dismissed without finesse, retired to his Paris flat and busied himself in work on the three volumes of his memoirs.

All this time there were the 400,000 French soldiers fastened up in the useless Maginot Line. And it was now, when all was lost, that some French troops really fought, and fought hard.

On 21 May it was agreed that the Royal Air Force should concentrate on the northern sector. From then on, Bomber Command put almost all its 500 aircraft in, and they were working almost without a pause. The Official History says that it was now that Fighter Command made 200 sorties a day, using all but ten of its entire total of squadrons. (These ten included the two squadrons in Norway, three night-fighter squadrons, and one non-operational squadron.) German reports said that it now had to be admitted that the Stukas had suffered heavy losses with the extra Royal Air Force influx, so, to the Germans, the air war had 'suddenly become critical'.

While it is easy to say that certain forces retreated or withdrew, these manoeuvres, made in war and in a hurry, are never tidy or systematic. Each plane scrambled home as best it could. But they got there: and could take a breath before Dunkirk. Now, as the Germans drove on towards the Channel coast, it would naturally become easier to attack them from England. But all that was apparent to the British Expeditionary Force was the increasing awareness that it was in terrible danger and that its air cover seemed to have disappeared.

On 16 May Rommel intended to break through the Maginot Line, as he thought it was. The Germans had believed French propaganda that the Line, which in fact stopped at Longwy, close to the south-west corner of Luxembourg, had been extended a good deal further along the Franco-Belgian frontier. All the French had done north of Longwy was to make, quickly during the winter, a line of pill-boxes and anti-tank obstacles, which had now been manned in a hurry by the remnants of the French Eleventh Corps. This had been having a rough time and, as a Corps, had almost ceased to exist. Rommel, however, believing that these scratch fortifications were as strong as the Line proper, took his time getting ready. When he set off, he was travelling as usual in the lead, in Colonel Rothenburg's command-tank. The Seventh Panzer met some resistance at Clairfayts, knocked out two pill-boxes and blew up any obstacles they could see, whereupon they had a gap which they could smash through. Rommel ordered the advance, and in full moonlight they sped foward. 'We'll do it like the Navy – fire salvos to port and starboard' – which they did. The French were caught off balance: it was against all the rules of warfare to go on by night. Rommel noted that his procession made such a racket that no one could have slept through it, and he also observed both refugees and French troops hiding in the ditches. He made straight for Avesnes, where his tanks came up with what was left of the French First Armoured, and there was a sharp action, several Panzers being disabled, and only three French tanks left to withdraw. As dawn began to lighten the sky, Rommel pressed on to Landrecies. If troops and refugees blocked the way, his tanks simply drove on to the grass and passed round them. One of his Commanders shouted to the French soldiers to lay down their arms, and, rather to his surprise, many did so. The Panzers crossed the bridge over the Sambre at Landrecies (scene of a small heroic British action in 1914) and only stopped when they were dangerously near to running out of petrol, on a slope near Le Cateau. From that night the place names Rommel saw were the old, memory-crowded scenes of the Great War, including Cambrai and Arras. He had come almost fifty miles in less than twenty-four hours. His path was no wider than the road he was on, and he had broken most of the rules of conventional warfare, but in less than two days he had lost one officer and fewer than forty other men, had disposed of 100 French tanks and counted more than 10,000 prisoners. He had also created panic and despair wherever he went. At Landrecies he had cut the line which the French had been told to hold at all costs, and the French Ninth Army was now no longer a fighting force. The whole exploit established his extraordinary reputation for good and all.

The Allied High Commands would have been astounded to know what nervous apprehensions were gripping some of the German leaders at this time. Von Rundstedt had never stopped worrying about his southern flank, and was haunted by the remembrance of von Kluck's fatal turn in 1914 when his Army had swept round above the Marne and presented Joffre with his great opportunity. Von Rundstedt saw it all happening again. Hitler himself, whose daring plan had frightened his old-style generals to death, was now markedly nervous about 'too far too fast'. On the other hand Halder, a professional soldier from cap to boot sole, was no longer the cautious thinker of a week before, but was brimming with confidence, writing in his diary that the campaign was developing into a classic. Reports from German Intelligence confirmed him, showing that French resistance was not apparent in key sectors, and that the French on the southern flank were too slight to mount a major attack. The truth was that the Germans did not yet realise that to all intents and purposes they had won. Hitler ordered a halt on 17 May, an order furiously resented by (for example) Guderian, but it had to be obeyed as it was a Führer-order, and it was true that the Panzer forces badly needed a rest: they had hardly stopped for a week and were dropping with fatigue.

The Luftwaffe needed a break too. They were using two big air fleets, Fleet Two under General Albert von Kesselring and Fleet Three under General Hugo Sperrle (who did not get on any too well with each other, for von Kesselring much admired Goering while Sperrle did not). Together the two Fleets consisted at the start of the campaign of 1,120 bombers, 324 dive-bombers, and 1,264 fighters, forming six Air Corps. Corps One and Four had been allocated to The Netherlands and Belgium, Corps Two and Five to north-east France, one was a Special Duty Corps for airborne operations, and Corps Eight, which included most of the dive-bombers and was to go wherever it could be of most use, was commanded by Lieutenant-General Wolfram von Richthofen, a cousin of the world-famous ace of the Great War. By mid-May these Air Fleets had suffered many losses, and were now operating at the extreme limits of their range. Their crews were in sore need of a rest. Goering, spending most of his time in his private train far from the battle-zones, was still cheerfully confident that his wonderful Luftwaffe could do anything, and declared that they could easily destroy the British Expeditionary Force: 'This is a special job for the Luftwaffe!' Hitler backed him up, equally ignorant of actual conditions. This decision was received with incredulous dismay by air and ground commanders alike, who after all were on the spot and knew what was happening in their sectors. Von Kesselring said that the destruction of the British Army was completely beyond the strength of the existing air forces. What was more, these air forces were dispersed all over the battle-zones: they were attacking St Quentin, Boulogne, Lille, Amiens, and above all Calais, leaving only small formations of Heinkel 111s and Junkers 88s to go for the retiring British and French. It would take time to re-group the rest, and when they were ready they were going to need a stronger fighter escort than hitherto. Von Richthofen said that unless the Panzers could get going at once 'the English will give us the slip. No one can seriously believe that we alone can stop them from the air'. But Goering did, and Hitler thought Goering must know, so the orders remained unchanged.

It is not quite fair to picture the French Army as demoralised and fleeing throughout. There were pockets of stout resistance and even attack, though these were too scattered to amount to much. One is of interest as it was a tank force, led by a soldier who had always believed in using tanks as spearheads, as Guderian did. His troops inflicted a few disagreeable surprises on the Germans during the pathetically few days they had to try in. The tanks were led by a forty-nine year old chain-smoker who was to become better known later: Colonel Charles de Gaulle. He had sensibly refused a place in Reynaud's War Cabinet, preferring action in the field. When he saw the chaos of retreat east of Laon, and heard that the Germans had told the French to throw down their weapons and get off the roads because 'we haven't time to take you prisoner', he was so angry that, as he wrote later, he was determined from that moment to fight on until the French disgrace was washed away. Everything he did after that, he said, sprang from what he saw that day.

His attacks were bold and intelligent, and surprised the Germans, but could not halt them, mainly because de Gaulle had no infantry support and no flank cover, but they were enough to make his name as a fine Commander and to persuade the Free French troops to follow him. Later they became part of his legend in France.

Broadhurst duly reported back to Dowding who, after hearing all he had to say, sent him to take command at Wittering where his Chief would again be Leigh-Mallory. Within a short time Dowding rang up and said he would like to come to luncheon. Broadhurst

immediately telephoned Leigh-Mallory on the assumption that he would be coming as well. It transpired that he knew nothing of the visit, but agreed that he ought to come. So I found myself at luncheon with the C-in-C on my right hand and the AOC on my left, wondering what it was all about. Nothing of much importance cropped up except, perhaps, the night-fighter squadron, which I had just had, being equipped with Radar – Dowding was very keen to have the night-fighter squadrons equipped and trained as soon as possible. At about two o'clock Leigh-Mallory asked to be excused. I saw him to his car.

When I came back to the table, Dowding immediately said, 'Broadhurst, if I offered you a Wing of Fighters to take to France, what would you say?' I stared at him, thinking he must have gone mad, and said, 'Well, of course I'd go, sir.' He said, 'Of course you would go, but what would you think? How successful do you think you would be?' I said, 'Well, I doubt if we'd last a week. No Radar, no proper telephones, and completely outnumbered.' He said, 'Thank you. That's all I wanted to know.' With that he got up and left.

It wasn't until after the War when I read the various despatches of Fighter Command that I realised what enormous moral pressure he was under from both the British and the French Governments to send more fighters to France to try to save it from collapse. He knew the real battle was to come, and he could not afford to send Fighter Squadrons in a lost cause.

It only later dawned on Broadhurst that his account, and his reaction, were what Dowding needed – the views of a man senior enough to have a commander's eye yet not too senior to perceive the unvarnished opinions of the men as a whole. It confirmed Dowding's inner certainty that the Royal Air Force would be very soon the vital part of the struggle to come, and to come soon. But first there was the matter of the British Expeditionary Force. It was quickly apparent that Broadhurst's

main job at Wittering was to operate my fighters from forward landing grounds for the defence of the evacuation at Dunkirk. To indicate the C-in-C's concern to conserve his fighters for the coming Battle of Britain, we were under strict orders not to operate Spitfires over Dunkirk unless they had been fitted with armour-plate.

Broadhurst, whose cherished 'HB' Hurricane had received a shell through its oil-tank so that he never did know how he had managed to get home in it, was rung up from Northolt by a polite voice telling him: 'Your Hurricane is ready for you, sir.' Delighted, he went to fetch it. 'Of course, Wittering was all Spitfires. They saw this HB Hurricane and just took it away. I was sorry about that.'

France, he said, was pure chaos. 'We learnt more about war in a few days there than we'd learnt in everything before then.'

Denis David echoes this and enlarges on it:

Our tactical manuals were really out of date for dealing with the Luftwaffe. Follow-ing their advice was too murderous, too many were killed that way, and the same was true of the idea of the 'big wing'. Tactics had to adapt, we had to learn to weave as the Germans did. Dowding and Park had it right. Park was marvellous, absolutely the right man in the right place at the right time. As for Dowding – well, it was obvious when he came to the reunions, even the late ones when he was in a wheel-chair. You could feel the waves of admiration and love going out to him.

One thing that materially helped Dowding in his struggle to hold on to his squadrons in England was that Barrett reported to Newall that at most he had room for only three more squadrons in France. By the time Newall received this report he had room for less than that, for he had to withdraw his aircraft from the River Aisne area to landing-fields near Troyes, moving his own Headquarters back at the same time. These moves were complicated by a lack of lorries, though this was less of a problem than it otherwise would have been because the Germans were not looking beyond the Aisne just then and because Barratt contrived to borrow (his word) 300 new American lorries from the French. At the same time Barratt's most depleted bomber squadrons went back to England, leaving six out of the ten, though these six were by no means complete. During the moves, the Royal Air Force had little chance of combat.

It is time to catch up with Parrott and his friends. They, like all Allied military units, were ill-informed. Information was scanty and unreliable; rumours were plentiful and ever-changing. On the evening of 16 May Parrott was told that he could take a rest day on the 17th.

However, I was woken by a friend at seven-thirty saying that he and I were going on leave, and there was an Avro Ensign airliner of the ATA waiting on the airfield to take us to England. It took him a little time to convince me. (The only explanation of this odd event is that we were the youngest and most junior of the squadron pilots, and were the only ones who had not had home leave since arriving in France, and someone in authority had decided that the leave roster must continue.) Expect-ing to return to the Squadron I took only an overnight bag, leaving the rest of my kit in my billet. We arrived at Hendon and reported to the Station Adjutant who, after telephoning the Air Ministry, issued us with leave passes for ten days and sent us on our way home.

Forty-eight hours later I received a telegram from the Air Ministry telling me to report to Number 145 Squadron at Tangmere. I expected to be taking a replacement aircraft to 607, but on arrival at Tangmere found that I was posted to the squadron there. I explained to the Squadron Commander that I had virtually only the clothes I stood up in, and please could I go up to London to get some replacements? [Parrott here uses a charming phrase] Thanks to Ali Burberry and the forty Gieves who, even in wartime, most generously gave extended credit to young Royal Air Force officers, in exchange for an everlasting monthly bankers' order, my immediate needs were met.

On 22 May I flew my first patrol with 145 – a sweep round the Lille-Arras area which I had so recently left, now occupied by Germans. Further patrols along the French coast, over Calais, Boulogne and Le Tréport, were made on the 23rd and 24th. On the 26th we did our first patrol over Dunkirk. The town was hidden under a pall of black smoke but, on the beaches, we could see clusters of troops, with

Navy vessels offshore. The following days showed much the same picture with the smoke from the burning oil tanks and other fires rising higher and higher.

In the evening of 26 May my aircraft was damaged by return fire from a Heinkel 111, and I made a forced landing with the wheels up when the engine stopped as I crossed the coast near Deal. Regrettably I hit two sheep as I skidded to a stop. The farmer's reaction was a measure of how little the two weeks of 'real' war, as opposed to the 'phony' war, had affected people even in the Dover area, and also how little they knew about the débâcle in France. I spent the night at Manston, and was flown back to Tangmere the next day in a Tiger Moth. I missed flying operationally that day but resumed the following day and continued until the end of the evacuation.

At this time fighter squadrons had an establishment of eighteen aircraft and there were about twenty pilots on strength including the Commanding Officer and the two Flight Commanders. The standing patrols over Dunkirk had resulted in 145 losing four pilots and nine aircraft. Other squadrons had suffered similar losses, so many of them could no longer provide the twelve aircraft at readiness which was expected of them. In those last few days the remaining members and aircraft were being combined to make up a composite squadron of twelve.

Aircraft were replaced quite quickly despite the heavy losses in France, but replacement pilots were not so plentiful, and it was not until the middle of July that we had a full complement again.

Many Royal Air Force pilots had to learn a lot in a very short time over Dunkirk. The first vital lesson was to fly high enough for the Luftwaffe not to jump them. They found that 12,000 feet was not high enough, so they went up to 14,000, which was still not jump-proof, whereupon they increased the height to 20,000. The next thing of cardinal importance was not to go in over the beaches. It would be far too late to intercept the German bombers if they did that. 'Catch them before they get there' was the advice they were given, and which they followed whenever possible, and this worked much better – but it meant, of course, that the British Expeditionary Force could not see them, which led to unfortunate and unjust recriminations later.

During Dunkirk, the Luftwaffe losses were assessed by the German High Command at 156. This figure included five aircraft not accredited to enemy action (which prompts some intriguing speculations), nor does it include nineteen which crashed at places far enough away to doubt whether they were engaged, or were intending to be engaged, in the Dunkirk area. The British claimed 262 enemy losses, which was certainly an exaggerated estimate. We have already seen how easy it is to assemble reports without being able to be perfectly certain that some claims have not, for example, been duplicated. But the really important fact, from the Royal Air Force point of view, was that the Luftwaffe, with its greater numbers and its fearsome reputation for carrying all before it, had not been able to dominate in the battles fought in, or round, the evacuation area.

These considerations apply to bombing activities as well. One Wing Commander was shot down on 27 May and unluckily landed on the wrong side of the German lines, so he had to make his way back as best he could, and it took him three weeks. The sight that struck him most forcibly on this difficult journey was that of a railway station and its marshalling-yards on the River Somme which had been bombed with what he called terrific damage. It reminded him of the bombing scenes in the film *Things To Come*. He did not say, and probably did not know, which side was responsible for this, but, judging by reports in general at the time, it was most likely to have been the Luftwaffe. On the other hand, records contain several references to the 'valuable work' done by Bomber Command on the Dunkirk approaches.

The British Expeditionary Force, either extricating itself piecemeal from Belgium or falling back as slowly as it dared in front of the Panzers, was being driven towards the sea. Now it was that its Commander suddenly emerged as the right man in the right place. He had never figured as a 'great' commander, not one for the history books, though he had a solid reputation. But now John Vereker, sixth Viscount Gort, was truly impressive. He was to outward appearances a British Guardsman bulldog, simple, straightforward, loyal and utterly unpretentious, but in the Great War he had had nine mentions in despatches, had won the Military Cross and the Victoria Cross, and he was much loved by his men. He was unquestioning in his obedience to orders, but he had seen how shaky the French were, how often a prey to panic, and he knew how fast the Germans must be moving to make the French fall back as they had, and he determined to save his Army.

He warned the War Office that it might come to evacuation. This was the typical English reaction to defeat – Gallipoli is a famous example – whereas the French instinct was always to retire into a fortress, as they did at Metz in 1870. The Chief of the Imperial General Staff, Field-Marshal Lord Ironside, arrived with an official order that Gort must fight his way through to the South. With seven of his nine divisions engaged in the North, Gort refused. Ironside accepted this and reported to London: 'Situation desperate. God help the BEF'. From the moment he heard of this, Vice-Admiral Sir Bertram Ramsay, the Flag Officer commanding at Dover, began to assemble shipping. Plans for fetching the Army home, given the title of Operation Dynamo, were quickly set in motion. Destroyers, sloops, corvettes, gunboats, minesweepers, drifters and trawlers, armed boarding-vessels, motor torpedo-boats, yachts with naval crews, barges, Thames tugs, lifeboats from liners anchored in London docks, fishing-boats and pleasure-boats, began to assemble. Boatyards yielded launches and motor-boats. As the news spread, mostly by word of mouth, volunteer boat-owners brought out their various craft, just as their ancestors had done when the Armada was sighted coming towards the Channel in 1588.

The British Expeditionary Force was falling back towards the port of Dunkirk, which faces a treacherous stretch of water. Wreckage has been found there for centuries. Eastward the sands, an unbroken sixteen-mile expanse as far as the mouth of the River Yser, form the longest continuous beach in Europe, with an average width of a mile. Three-quarters of a mile out from the low-water mark is a deep channel, the Rade de Dunquerque, half a mile wide and forty to fifty feet deep. Nowhere is there any pier or jetty except at Dunkirk itself, where at that time there were two, a jetty west of the harbour, and the East Mole, a narrow wooden structure 1400 yards long and about five feet broad, along which many of the escaping soldiers were to go. Curiously enough it survived every attempt, whether by the Luftwaffe or by the German artillery, to destroy it.

As the British reached Dunkirk, they began to build what was known as the perimeter, a defensive wall encircling the town. It was made up of any material to hand: smashed lorries and cars, stones, sandbags, rubble from bombed buildings which became more plentiful as time went on. Alongside them was a sizeable contingent of the French First Army, which had come along beside them as the Belgian Army began to crumble and who were of the greatest help in consolidating the defensive positions. On the night of 26 May, Calais fell. This left a fair-sized section of the Luftwaffe free to go for Dunkirk, which they did at dawn on the 27th, dropping bombs on the port to such effect that by a quarter-past seven the harbour was blocked and the centre of the town was what those who saw it described as a blazing shambles. That day Belgium surrendered. Now the Allied soldiers in their cul-de-sac, with the sea the only way out, presented the Luftwaffe with an ideal target. The soldiers on the beaches were sitting ducks. Well-informed people referred to earlier examples of the annihilation of ground forces by air forces in 1918, the Turks in the Beisan gorge, the Bulgarians in the Struma defile, the Austrians after Vittorio Veneto, all at minuscule cost in aircraft. Surely the Luftwaffe could now put these exploits in the shade.

But none of the trapped victims of 1918 had had the sea behind them. And they had not had the French First Army, which heroically covered the evacuation from the land, standing between the Germans and the beaches, fighting, as the Germans found, for every house and every foot of ground. This was how the French were expected to fight, how they had always fought. This was la gloire as it was traditionally understood. Why had other divisions been so different?

No one at Dunkirk was asking this then, partly because they did not know about the débâcle elsewhere, partly because they had plenty of other things to think about. The sea played its part too. For once the uncertain-tempered English Channel chose to be calm, and a total of 861 ships, the most motley lot ever seen, came across, some of them going back and forth for nine days, the smaller ones coming right up to the beaches and going back and forth to the bigger ones, taking the soldiers off. John Masefield called it the Nine Days' Wonder, and described the long patient lines waiting on the sands before wading out to the boats. Soon after the evacuation began, Churchill warned the House of Commons to prepare itself for hard and heavy tidings, and told the War Cabinet in a deliberately off-hand tone that of course whatever happened at Dunkirk we should fight on. He remarked afterwards that if at that point he had shown the least doubt or hesitation he would have been hurled out of office at once.

If Guderian and Rommel had been left to make their own speed throughout, it could never have worked: but once again an attack of cold feet had made Hitler order another pause. So the German armour, which had pressed on to Boulogne and Calais, again had to halt. The principal reason for this was a vigorous and morale-raising push on 21 May at Arras by a small British force and a few French units, both with some tanks. They advanced ten miles and, though losing a number of tanks and men, gave an impression out of all proportion to their strength. It was of course Rommel's men they engaged, who were temporarily checked. The main effect of this attack was to cause

Back from action. Spitfire aircraft with flaps down coming in to land.

von Rundstedt once more to ask Hitler to call a halt. By the evening of 23 May Guderian had come in sight of both Calais and Boulogne, while Rommel, having regrouped, had pushed on to the Lorette Heights (site of the great French Military Cemetery, where a Great War monument proclaimed that 'who holds the Lorette Heights holds France', and faces that other memory-laden crest, Vimy Ridge). Rommel's advance guard was at the gates of Béthune and his motorised infantry, along with the Luftwaffe, were assaulting Lens. Not until the twenty-fifth did Boulogne fall, while the British at Calais held out valiantly until a day later. The Panzers, then poised along the Aa Canal ready to dash for Dunkirk, were stopped by the imperative Führer Order for two crucial days – days that made the British Army's escape possible.

Despite its losses, the Luftwaffe still greatly outnumbered the Royal Air Force, and moreover had French airfields close at hand from which to operate. The Royal Air Force had to fly from home and back and therefore had less time to spend in the battle-zone, but for the first time in the war they were able to concentrate on one place at one time in clearly defined terms. Coastal Command joined in, making 171 sorties with its Blenheims, Hudsons and Skuas, along with a few Rocs borrowed from the Fleet Air Arm. The Blenheims went for German troops by day. Bomber Command bombed roads and rear communications by night in 651 sorties. But Fighter Command was still in the centre of the picture. Now at last some of the cherished Spitfires came into the battle, proving their value, and the mettle of their relatively inexperienced pilots, from the start. Figures of 'scores' were daily reported. These figures are, as we know, notoriously hard to compute, partly because they do not as a rule include aircraft on either side that have somehow managed to struggle back to base, where the damage may prove to be so severe that the machines have to be written-off.

On 27 May the Luftwaffe made twelve heavy attacks on Dunkirk, using a total of 300 bombers and 550 fighters. 15,000 high explosive and 30,000 incendiary bombs were dropped. They reported a loss of twenty-three bombers. The Royal Air Force claimed thirty-eight German aircraft shot down. Fourteen Spitfires and Hurricanes were lost, but many more limped back home riddled with bullet-holes. 54 Squadron had only six serviceable Spitfires left when it returned to Hornchurch. All three Biggin Hill squadrons had been in action, 610 (Spitfires) and 213 and 242 (Hurricanes). 610 shot down a Heinkel, but as it fell the pilot managed to fire his Véry signals, which brought forty Messerschmidt 109s to the scene, odds of more than three to one. The Spitfires shot down three and claimed three 'probables', and lost one of their number. They were particularly annoyed because on the way home they saw a big formation of Junkers 87 and 88 and could do nothing about it, having no ammunition left. The two Hurricane squadrons met ten Messerschmidt 109s and shot down two without loss to themselves.

56 (Hurricane) Squadron left Manston at half-past three in the afternoon to patrol the St Omer-Calais area and shot down two Heinkels and one 'possible'. Maxwell, having accounted for one of the Heinkels, was himself shot down, and had to bale-out. He took fourteen minutes to descend, and landed in a ring of soldiers with rifles. They turned out to be Belgian, but their officer was highly suspicious. No wonder, Maxwell thought – he was wearning a shabby old tunic and carrying no identity discs or papers. He explained this, whereupon the soldiers laughed and hugged him and the officer said: 'You must be English, only the English would go to war like that'. At that moment a big car drew up, another officer got out and joined them. When he heard the story he asked Maxwell to come over to the car, where Prince Charles of the Belgians would like to see him. It turned out that the Prince knew Maxwell's family, having stayed with them in Scotland. He was most affable, produced another car, a driver, and a pass and sent Maxwell off to Ostend. There he watched two Stuka attacks, and at half-past ten that night got on board a trawler. A little way off-shore the trawler was fired at by an E-boat, but, thanks to the trawler's shallow draught, the torpedoes passed harmlessly underneath it and the trawler tied up safely at Deal the following morning.

It was somewhere about this time that David had what he called his oddest, and funniest, experience. Six Hurricanes of 87 Squadron, one of which was his, had flown on a patrol over Belgium and had shot down fourteen Junkers 87. They had all run out of ammunition and were turning for home. Not far from Louvain David noticed another Hurricane, of 85 Squadron this time, which had also run out of ammunition: 'and there was a Messerschmidt 109 creeping up on him. So I dived between them and the Messerschmidt sheered off. He never realised he'd run away from two empty Hurricanes.' When the Squadron Commander heard about it he roared with laughter.

David won his DFC in May and the Bar to it in June. In his opinion

> experience is the thing – by August we'd take four Hurricanes out against three
> hundred and think nothing of it. The vital thing was to have not only operational
> pilots but *experienced* operational pilots.
>   Once you've killed a pilot it does something to you, just as when you've seen the
> Germans strafing a road full of refugees. You can see for yourself if you look at
> photographs of carefree young men who become thoughtful when they've seen
> what it was like.

The weather was heavily overcast throughout 28 May and the morning of the 29th,
making bombing difficult and accurate bombing impossible. Then came pouring rain
with a cloud base down to 300 feet. While German Commanders miles away kept
asking for attacks, those on the spot knew perfectly well that having to fly so low would
expose the Luftwaffe to well-aimed storms of flak from the armed British ships
offshore, which could, and did when tried, cause more German losses than the
Germans were inflicting on the British, even allowing for the German fighters making
beach-runs to rake the waiting troops with machine-gun fire. This was something the
young Luftwaffe pilots hated doing: firing at a plane, or bombing a building, was one
thing, but this was quite another. The older, more hardened German officers were not
as hardened as all that either: 'it was an awful sight if you looked too closely'.

The weather cleared in the afternoon, and at a quarter to three 180 Stukas attacked
in three waves, followed forty-five minutes later by powerful bomber assaults on the
shipping. These damaged seven destroyers and sank three, and sank five passenger
ships too. Of course, as close to the coast as that, many of the men on board could
get back on shore, but it was hard to have come so near to getting away and have to
begin, so to speak, all over again. The Royal Air Force made nine patrols to intercept
the attack-waves, and shot down fourteen, losing sixteen themselves.

The thirtieth of May opened with rain and mist, and when the rain stopped the mist
thickened into fog which persisted until next day. The Luftwaffe stood ready but could
not take off: it was midday on 31 May before the weather was clear enough, and by
then the Luftwaffe was working with smaller numbers. They did manage to sink a
freighter and to damage six destroyers, but this was a much slighter achievement than
they had managed before. The Royal Air Force flew nine patrols and shot down
seventeen German aircraft. At the same time Blenheims of Number Two Group, along
with six French aircraft (which had flown from Cherbourg across to Tangmere to
refuel and take on bombs), attacked the Dunkirk perimeter – a welcome sight to the
hard-pressed troops. After successfully dropping their bombs they all withdrew, four
of them to Cherbourg and the rest back to England, where by now every south-eastern
airfield was packed with an astonishing assortment of aircraft. This mixture was
reflected in some of their sorties. At dusk a motley collection – Blenheims, Ansons of
Coastal Command, Fairey Albacores and Blackburn Skuas of the Fleet Air Arm –
returned to attack the German troop-formations. Ansons and Hudson reconnaissance-
bombers of Coastal Command began what came to be called The Sands Patrol, flying
at their slow speed over the beaches and shipping, with their air-crews displaying great

gallantry in taking on larger enemy forces. Some of the Ansons had been hurriedly fitted with machine-guns in their side windows, which gave an unpleasant surprise to the Messerschmidts, three at least of which they shot down.

Someone had come up with the idea of sending two Skua target-tugs, brought from Gosport to Detling near Maidstone, to fly at night over the water, patrolling a straight course ten miles out from Dunkirk. Here they would at fairly regular intervals drop flares so that it would be possible to spot any German Navy ships that might be near-by. The flares, more than twenty for each target-tug, were of 20,000 candle-power and burnt brilliantly for more than three minutes. Of course this made the target-tugs highly visible as well. One Skua pilot said it was like flying inside an electric light bulb, with the added disadvantage that the spray thrown up by the flare-tube hitting the water and then exploding misted the windows so that he was flying blind and dazzled for minutes at a time.

Saturday 1 June dawned clear and sunny, so the Luftwaffe threw in everything it had, opening with forty dive-bombers screeching down at first light. As they turned away, the supporting Messerschmidts were engaged by twenty-eight Hurricanes which dispersed them. Three Hudsons claimed three, while three Ansons of 501 Squadron took on nine Messerschmidts, destroying two and claiming two 'probables'. Fighter Command made eight patrols with a reported 'kill' of forty-three. The Luftwaffe sank four destroyers and ten other craft and admitted a loss of twenty-nine with thirteen damaged.

By this time the British had grown more cunning. The evacuation was mostly proceeding by night. The British soldiers had improvised an extra jetty out of Army trucks with planks laid between them. It brought the men closer to the waiting boats and gave them an extra place to hide in daylight.

Sunday, rather surprisingly, was a good deal quieter. It seems that the Luftwaffe had been told to make ready for Operation Paula, a strong air assault on industrial plant and airfields in the neighbourhood of Paris. There was only one real air-raid at Dunkirk, at eight in the morning, when 120 bombers were met and broken up by five Spitfire and Hurricane squadrons. Two ships were damaged. Apart from that there were a few attacks on Allied troops on the perimeter. One German pilot baled out of his Junkers 88 and landed on the beach, where he picked himself up to face a bunch of armed grim-faced soldiers. He sensibly put up his hands and, surrounded by his captors, crouched in a foxhole in the dunes for the rest of the day, while from time to time German artillery shells exploded on the sands, sometimes unpleasantly close. At dusk the whole party moved down to the makeshift jetty. The German pilot knew that his escape was now or never. He edged deliberately to the side of the queue, taking his time, and noticed that his captors were staggering with fatigue. At what seemed a suitable moment he jumped into the water. The sound of shots dimly reached him but had stopped by the time he came up to the surface. Inch by inch he worked his way back under the jetty, where he hid, most uncomfortably and up to his neck in water, for the rest of the night.

On Monday only von Richthofen's dive-bombers appeared. The rest of the Luftwaffe was busy south of the Somme in the warm-up for Operation Paula. The German artillery, however, went on firing shells at the beaches and, they hoped, the shipping. The enemy pilot was safe and undiscovered, to his surprise. He was, though, suffering acutely from hunger and – worse – thirst, made more tormenting by his soaked condition and the salt water lapping round him. He stayed there until nearly dawn next day, 4 June, when he began carefully to draw himself back up the beach until he was finally clear of the water. All was still. The sun came up, warm and clear, the shells still fell, but at ten o'clock he slowly ventured out, and stared incredulously at the beaches, empty except for abandoned equipment. The sea was empty too. He sank down on the warm sand and slept until, later in the day, some German soldiers found him, after which, as far as he was concerned, all was well.

Dunkirk was full of odd incidents that etched themselves on the minds of the men who saw them. Five Messerschmidt 109s flying in a defensive circle round a Spitfire circling the other way inside the ring, the English pilot almost helpless with laughter. One Hurricane pilot looking in vain for the sight of the familiar roundel and, catching sight of another Hurricane at last, pairing up with it: its pilot, anticipating (no doubt like many others) the 1943 comment of Guy Gibson's bomb-aimer Spafford on low-level flying practice over English lakes, remarked through his microphone: 'This is bloody dangerous'. Two Hurricanes shot down a Junkers 88 which crippled one of them, the two crashed into the sea together and both pilots wriggled out. Wading in the water, they were only yards apart, so they struggled ashore together. They were very close to the German lines, so the Junkers pilot, who was barefoot, cheerfully claimed his prisoner, commandeered a big Belgian car and drove his prize to Bruges, where he was officially declared a prisoner of war.

Some shot-down pilots became mixed up with refugees on the outskirts of Dunkirk. One, who had scrambled out of his wrecked Hurricane a moment before it went up in flames on the coast fifteen miles from the port, cadged a lift for part of the way, pinched a bicycle and only abandoned it when the road was too crammed with people to do anything but walk. When he reached the beach it was a sight he would never forget. The waiting soliders were reeling with fatigue but they could still get to what cover there was when the enemy aircraft came in low. Many soldiers flung themselves into the water and stayed with their heads just showing until the raiders had passed. The pilot managed to get into a rescue-ship and was safely landed at Dover.

Two Spitfire pilots watched a destroyer break in half and sink in seconds. One of them later said that the scene at Dunkirk 'defied description'. A Junkers pilot remarked that he and his friends thought it was hell: 'We met terrific resistance from the British fighters and the battleship anti-aircraft guns'. Lacking battle experience or not, the mettle of the Royal Air Force was clearly seen. Within a few days of the start of the evacuation, the German bombers were beginning to jettison their bombs regardless of where they fell, and flying off instead of picking out targets, and the German fighters seemed to have lost their fine cutting edge. The smoke from Dunkirk's bombed buildings blew westwards across the Channel, people in Sussex could smell it and British pilots said that anyone could fly straight from Brighton to Dunkirk simply by following the dark smoke trail.

Royal Air Force losses, including aircraft seriously damaged, were seventy-one out of 822 sorties for Bomber Command and, for Fighter Command, 106 out of 2,739 sorties. They claimed 262 German aircraft, and the Royal Navy claimed thirty-five. The Germans said that their total losses were 240, 132 of them at Dunkirk itself. Analysis of losses in all Commands of the Royal Air Force pointed to various contributory causes: the greater enemy numbers, the ever-changing scene, the accuracy of German anti-aircraft fire, the difficulty of finding targets obscured by smoke and flame, and the vulnerability of the Battles and Blenheims. There was the added problem of nursing damaged aircraft home over the Channel which under such conditions seemed to take for ever, as German pilots were to find out later. It is true that by 4 June, the end of Dunkirk, British fighter defences were at their lowest point. Dowding wrote in a despatch that when the evacuation was complete he had only three squadrons which had not been engaged in day-fighting across the Channel, and twelve of his squadrons had been engaged for the second time after having been withdrawn to re-form. He particularly regretted losing machines which had been under repair in France and had to be abandoned there. Over the next two weeks the last few British aircraft in France came home, their ground staff going by sea from French ports so far uncaptured.

It was probably Dunkirk that really brought home to the Royal Air Force what a noisy business war is. For at Dunkirk the long-range shells were concentrated in one area. Film clips exist showing the large number of soldiers needed to fire one of these huge guns, jumping back and putting their fingers in their ears as the assigned man pulls the firing-cord. On top of those earth-shaking bangs and the crash of falling masonry came the long rattle of machine-gun fire from ground and air, the screech of the diving Stukas, the detonation of bombs and the thunder of tumbling debris. Moving tanks made their own din, burning buildings and vehicles made their own roar. Noise is an assault in itself, and, if there are also clouds of dust and smoke and flashes of fire, it is not surprising that impressions are confused, or that battles are basically a matter of managing as best one can, improvising from minute to minute as they go on, half deafened and unable to pick out many details among the chaos.

But the Army got away. 338,226 soldiers were brought safe home (though for 26,175 of them 'home' meant 'abroad', for they were Frenchmen). It is not so often remembered, but by the 18 June another 194,870 had joined them, 144,171 of them British, from French ports on the Atlantic coast. In those terrible days it was only right for those who could get away to do so, for it is always better to live to fight another day, and if the Army had been lost the war would probably have been lost as well. But it is never agreeable to think of, then or later, in the light of the long captivity upon which so much of Western Europe was entering. Paris fell on 14 June, and on the 17th the French Government, which had removed itself to Tours, asked for an armistice, which was concluded five days afterwards, on the 22nd.

It was by a narrow margin indeed that the Dunkirk 'miracle' took place. And what made it possible was the large number of ships, big and small, and what Philip Guedalla called the indomitable rearguard in the sky. Without Fighter Command, the brave ships could not have pulled it off. Without the ships, Fighter Command could not have managed it. The rescued Army owed its lives to both, and it needed all three Services to win the War.

Air Ministry reports from Dunkirk, saying that it was difficult to say exactly how effective the Royal Air Force was, with such remarks as 'inflicted greater losses than it suffered but could not prevent all bombings' and 'causing severe losses of Lysanders with little to show for it' (on 22 and 23 May respectively), are countered by a signal from the Senior Naval Officer at Dunkirk to the Vice-Admiral at Dover, sent at a quarter to eleven at night on the 28th, saying that fighter protection had been invaluable.

An example of an actual combat report might well be given here. These combat reports were typed on special sheets of paper, with a printed section at the top and space below. The top part consisted of twelve lines for details: the Sector Serial Number, the Serial Number of the Order for the patrol (which was not always filled in), the date, the Flight and Squadron, the number of enemy aircraft and their type or types, the time and place of attack, the casualties on both sides. Then, in the space provided, followed the General Report. On 2 June Flights A and B of 66 Squadron (this means six aircraft in two groups of three) estimated between thirty and forty enemy aircraft, Messerschmidt 109s, Junkers 88s, and Heinkel 111s, between half-past eight and a quarter to nine in the morning over Dunkirk, with the enemy flying from 16,000 feet to ground level. Two Junkers and two Messerschmidts were shot down and one 'probable' Heinkel, though the word 'probable' does not appear in the subsequent paragraph. Three British aircraft and one missing airman were Royal Air Force casualties.

The action was led by Squadron Leader R H A Leigh from Martlesham Heath on orders to patrol Dunkirk, and to the end of the normal patrol-time had not seen the enemy. At about half-past eight, however, they saw five Junkers 88s flying at 11,000 feet above a thin layer of cloud, and shot down two of them. Then they saw the Heinkels, with the Messerschmidt escort weaving round them, making bombing-runs over Dunkirk, and, in a number of individual attacks, destroyed a Heinkel and two Messerschmidts and damaged another Heinkel. Three British aircraft were a total loss, though the one casualty among the airmen was Flight Sergeant Hayman posted as missing.

The report ends with a comment somewhat surprising to the lay reader for a date in summer. 'All pilots experienced difficulty owing to frost forming on the inside of their windscreens when coming down to a low altitude. It is suggested that some form of inside heater be adopted.'

On Waterloo Day, 18 June, 73 Squadron was at Nantes, making preparations to leave France. In the morning the Commanding Officer had made a low-flying reconnaissance round Angers, north of Le Mans, and Tours, having seen, as he pleasantly reported, nothing more interesting than a group of 'agitated female cyclists' who rode their bicycles into a ditch as he approached, mistaking his Hurricane for a German aircraft. At half-past one in the afternoon all but six of the Squadron took off and patrolled the area for an hour before flying away to Tangmere. At a quarter to two the transport aircraft left, followed, a quarter of an hour later, by all the remaining serviceable French aircraft. There were eight unserviceable British aircraft – six Hurricanes, a Battle, and a Harrow on the airfield, and these were then set on fire.

The remaining ground staff were by this time ready to leave in the other Harrow.

It is well known to members of the armed services that the Non-Commissioned Officers, especially the Sergeants, have a well-deserved reputation for imperturbable, sensible conduct at moments of stress. One NCO submitted a most engaging report which illustrates this, as well as indicating the kind of last-minute actions that are characteristic on such occasions. As a final kindly gesture, he gave a Hotchkiss saloon staff car as a parting present to the café proprietor 'at the corner of the 'drome' who had been particularly generous in giving the Squadron food and coffee when their rations had failed to arrive. Just as this transaction was completed, an agitated Flight Lieutenant who was also an Intelligence Officer taxied up in a panic, shouting at the men to get away at once, as the Panzers were coming. That, in the opinion of the NCO, was all very well, but their Motor Transport driver was away up the road 'trying to sell an Austin Seven'. So he calmly remarked that there was plenty of time yet. 'Well, that did it. He handed me a torrent of abuse that I really couldn't listen to.' The NCO sent someone to fetch the missing driver and, upon the driver's return (we are not told whether the sale was completed), they all piled into the Harrow and left. The rest of the Squadron followed, and all got safely back to Tangmere.

General Erhard Milch was a quiet man whose personality was heavily overshadowed by that of his Chief, Goering, but who in fact had done far more to create the Luftwaffe than Goering had. During the Battle of France it was Milch's regular practice to fly over various areas of activity during the day and report back to Goering in his special train in the evening. On the fifth of June Milch flew over Dunkirk. That evening he found Goering smiling broadly at the British débâcle, as he called it. But Milch had seen what he had seen: the town in ruins, streets full of abandoned and smashed vehicles, the hulks of sunken ships sticking up out of the shallow water, and vast quantities of equipment, kit and personal belongings thickly strewn all over the beaches. But he had seen few dead soldiers – perhaps twenty or thirty, he said. Yes, it was a great reverse, but the British Army had got clean away, they were on the far side of the Channel by now. Equipment could be quickly replaced, 300,000 men could not. It was a great achievement, no doubt about that.

This, said Milch firmly, was Germany's opportunity. This very day, he emphasised, all the units of the Luftwaffe's Air Fleets Two and Three must be moved up to the coast, and they should go over at once, seize several vital airfields in the south-east of England with their paratroops and follow up quickly with squadrons of Stukas and Messerschmidts to operate from these captured airfields, just as they had done in Norway. Then the German Navy could carry troops across, but the Luftwaffe had several hundred transport aircraft which could go ahead of the ships, packed with two or three Army divisions and escorted by a strong force of fighter planes. It would be risky, for the transport aircraft could take no armour and no big guns, but the British could do little or nothing for a few days any way. Now was the time. If we leave them alone for a few weeks, he said presciently, it would be too late.

Goering demurred. According to what he reported later, he told Milch that he had only one paratroop division, and there had been difficulties in hanging on to that, let alone getting the four paratroop divisions he wanted, because the demands of the Army were being met first. Milch did not, then or later, blame Goering, and he voiced few criticisms of the Army, but he did blame Admiral Raeder, who seemed unduly hesitant. Of course Milch was not taking into account the full extent of the German naval losses in the Norwegian campaign. He had put forward his suggestion, and that was the best he could do. But, as June went on, and he visited one after another of the German or German-occupied airfields, he was increasingly perturbed to see no invasion preparations anywhere.

He did receive one reward, which gave him great pride. When Goering was made Reichsmarschall, Milch was promoted to Field Marshall (equal to Hindenburg! he reflected), a rank which could never be lost or retired from, which by an ordinance over sixty years old gave him precedence over ministers and, at any rate on paper, the Chancellor himself, and guaranteed for life full pay, an office with a staff officer and clerk just for him, and a supply of motors and horses for his personal use. Until the end of the Nuremberg trials he wore his Field Marshal's uniform. It might seem a poor consolation, but he made the most of it.

One unfortunate aspect of Dunkirk has already been touched on. It arose from the fact that soldiers only believe in air cover that they can actually see. Many of the invaluable and heroic Royal Air Force sorties had of necessity been out of sight of the troops on the beaches. So the rescued soldiers often felt bitter, and said so – 'Where were you all the time?' Knowing this, Churchill made a special point of commenting, as part of his famous 'we shall never surrender' speech to the House of Commons on 4 June, the day Dunkirk ended:

> We must be very careful not to assign to this deliverance the attributes of a victory. *Wars are not won by evacuations.* But there was a victory inside this deliverance, which should be noted. It was gained by the Air Force. Many of our soldiers coming back have not seen the Air Force at work; they saw only the bombers which escaped its protective attack. They underrate its achievement.

And then he added, with a remarkable touch of prophecy:

> The great French Army was very largely, for the time being, cast back and disturbed by the onrush of a few thousands of armoured vehicles. May it not also be that the cause of civilisation itself will be defended by the skill and devotion of a few thousand airmen?

5

Inside the Moat

In June 1940, and the months that followed, Britain stood in greater peril than at any moment in its history, knew it, and rather liked it.

Philip Guedalla

A lot of re-thinking was now necessary in the Royal Air Force. Some squadron commanders who had already foreseen this decided to act upon it. To do so was easier for those appointed to a fresh command, for they were new brooms. What they did was to assemble the entire squadron, ground and air, and talk to them, making them think over Dunkirk and all that had happened, what had been done that worked or had not worked, asking them to consider and discuss among themselves and see what conclusions they came to. Most men welcomed this: analysis of such a kind was new to them, and helpful. In addition there was as much fresh training as could be managed. New or still unpractised flying men were sent into the air with flight commanders, and the squadron commander himself organised practice dog-fights with himself as target. Experienced sergeant pilots would lead a flight until one of the officers was experienced enough to take over. Sometimes when this happened the former pupil would prove to be a star: as when Sergeant Richard Kilner took on a new Pilot Officer whose name became legendary, Paddy Finucane.

The normal person to lead a flight was a Squadron Leader, but if, as had to happen at times, however irksome this might be, he was busy with administration work, a flight commander would take his place. For far too long the standard (textbook) formation had been four vics of three aircraft each, the four making a diamond pattern in the sky. As we know, the German fighters flew more loosely, and this was plainly more practical: in any event once battle was joined it was every man for himself. Sooner or later each pilot had the weird experience of being carried miles on by battle momentum, so that one minute he was surrounded by aircraft and the next he was on his own with nothing in sight.

Now that what fighter action there was had been restricted to England and the Channel, pilots were increasingly eager for combat. They shared Maxwell's viewpoint, that Germans taking up space in English air were trespassing, those green fields and hills were theirs by centuries of right and not to be flown over, much less assaulted, by a lot of interfering foreigners. The sooner these intruders were forced to clear out the better. But it might take time. The Germans still had more aircraft, and, as they

77

were the aggressors, they could pick and choose where and when to attack. One pilot said that it was like playing tennis when the other person always had the serve, and all you could do was to return serve if you could, according to where he placed the ball.

The Dutch, Belgian and French airmen who had contrived to get away to the British Isles found it rather easier to settle down than did the Poles and Czechs. There had been long-standing connexions with the Dutch – had they not given us a king in 1688, for example? – and any Belgian, especially if he came from any place north of Brussels, had Anglo-Belgian co-operation implanted in his soul from 1914 if not before. And there were plenty of English people who had travelled to France in peace time and had learnt to love many features of French life: even those who could not understand why people made such a fuss about all that over-elaborate French food could appreciate good-looking farms, or splendid buildings, or flourishing orchards, or, if nothing else, the Mediterranean coast. And the Scots were old allies of the French. But hardly anyone in Great Britain before 1938 had set eyes on a Czech, or before 1939 a Pole, and these took some getting used to. The Poles were almost all airmen, as the air had been the only escape-route to the West in September 1939, so they joined the Royal Air Force. They proved to be courteous, punctilious in saluting and tigers of bravery in battle, but there were problems of other kinds. They enjoyed uproariously drink-laden parties, they invited ladies into their quarters, and, since a number of them were stationed in Scotland, they did, as one eminent writer charmingly pointed out, play old hob with the Scotch birth-rate. In addition, and this was a particular source of worry to the Royal Air Force, the punishments they inflicted on their own men for any dereliction of duty were not only unacceptably savage but, in the British Isles, illegal. British officers knew this and said so, they had no choice but to make the point clear. Also, the Poles had been in battle in Poland and rather naturally thought they knew all about it already, but the rule was that the squadron leader had to be British and, since he was the squadron leader, the rest must take their orders from him, like it or lump it.

One squadron leader had a very welcome stroke of luck in this respect. On their first day of operations the squadron scrambled and soon encountered a Junkers 88. After some hide and seek in and out of cloud, the squadron leader fired one burst, whereupon the Junkers vanished into the clouds again and, on the squadron's landing back at their airfield, it was discovered that that one burst of firing had shot the Junkers down, killing the pilot. The Poles acclaimed the squadron leader as a dead shot. He for his part had some trouble concealing his own astonishment. He had never even seen a German plane in flight before, so what he had done was pure luck, but it had given him such an advantage in prestige that he could never have admitted it.

The Czechs were found to be less intransigent than the Poles. They formed 310 Squadron which had a huge age range – their Commanding Officer was forty-five, far older than the English veterans who were still short of thirty, and the rest were mostly youngsters, some still barely out of their teens. But they looked trim and attractive in their dark blue uniforms with plenty of gold braid, they were well-disciplined and they got on well. On training flights they showed up excellently, except

Czech Fighter Squadron. On his return from his mission this pilot is met by the squadron mascot.

for one man who admitted that he had never actually piloted a plane as he was only a navigator. But they resembled the Poles in one thing. They had all seen their country invaded and occupied, and their great dream was to see it set free. Yet even in this there was a significant difference. Czechoslovakia had been taken over without a fight, no bombs had fallen on Prague, and Czech casualties throughout the War amounted to about 100,000. Warsaw, on the other hand, lay in ruins, and Poland lost two million of its people.

After France fell, all the Germans had to do to find convoys in the Channel was to take up a suitable position on the cliffs opposite Kent and look through their binoculars. And where there were convoys, there was Fighter Command. It seemed simple enough. But the British military commanders and the War Cabinet had thought about it too, and they decided a better scheme would be for the convoys to go round the other way. They recommended all shipping coming into the Western Approaches to alter course and sail up through St George's Channel and the Irish Sea to other ports, Liverpool or Glasgow perhaps. Many ships, but by no means all, did this. By now, the part of Kent bordering the Channel's narrowest point was referred to as 'Hellfire Corner'. South-eastern England was naturally the main target, and Dowding was determined to keep a fighter force there big enough to meet whatever came, but he would not leave the rest of the country wide open. It would be highly likely for the Luftwaffe to strike elsewhere, especially if they believed that every fighter squadron in England was rallying in the south-east. (They kept on hopefully saying "There can't be fifty Spitfires left by now'.) So Dowding made sure that the rest of the country had its squadrons still. This had its own advantage: squadrons in unattacked areas could relieve those under heavy pressure which would benefit by a little time to repair, re-fit and, if necessary, re-form.

The Luftwaffe in the meantime was attacking convoys wherever they could find them and dropping mines in British harbours. In a way it was easier to drop mines from aircraft than from mine-laying ships, which were larger and slower. A Junkers 88 could carry a thousand-pound mine under each wing, and could drop these pre-cisely in the regular shipping channels leading into harbours. The mines had to be dropped from low levels to prevent their parachutes from splitting open. There were snags of course. Ports and harbours, obvious objectives, were all protected by barrage balloons and anti-aircraft guns, as well as by ships' guns. It is, however, true that during the war as a whole the Luftwaffe destroyed more ships with mines than they did with bombs.

Most important of all, the Luftwaffe could now bomb the English airfields, with their ground staffs, Ops Rooms, aircraft on the ground with any luck, and their radio and Radar equipment. This might make a crucial difference, as both Air Forces were now having to bring in new inexperienced pilots and air-crews to replace the ones who had been lost. It was therefore a matter of learning fast. As one seasoned pilot expressed it, you were either lucky or dead.

When France had fallen, the rest of the world read the lesson of the past few weeks and were perfectly justified, living as they did outside these islands, in believing that it was only a matter of time. Perhaps only a few more weeks, and then Great Britain would have joined the majority – in both senses, they expected. But such a notion simply did not occur to any of the British themselves. Many observers have com-mented, often with an almost pained astonishment, on the surprising demeanour of the British when they were left alone. They did not feel defeated, they thought they were very likely to survive, somehow even to win in the end. Why not? 'The British always win the last battle'. Was that so fantastic? They were an island people and felt protected by their 'Moat', as Churchill was wise enough to call it. Not for nearly nine hundred years had they seen an invader's camp-fires on their soil. And they were curiously relieved to know that there was no one left to let them down. Every human being instinctively mistrusts the foreigner, even if the foreigner is foreign merely because he comes from a village ten miles away and has only lived in this one for thirty years. And island people depend on ships, and the Royal Navy was the Senior Service. David Low's celebrated cartoon showing a British soldier standing on a sea-girt rock and shaking a defiant fist at a stormy sky with approaching bombers and captioned 'Very well – alone' exactly suited their mood. They were friendly, too. Foreign observers who had been in England before noticed with surprise that the English were actually talking to one another in trains and on the bus, how an easy friendliness was apparent everywhere, most of all in the south-east, which was now in truth the new

80

front line. Literally so: for people standing on the cliffs at Dover did not need binoculars to see the coast at Calais, and were reassuringly reminded of the opposing extremes between the bond and the free.

Nowhere was the new situation more wholeheartedly welcome than at Bentley Priory. But it was for individual and special reasons. 'Thank God we're alone now' was Dowding's heartfelt response as he knew that no longer need he fear requests to send his fighters to help a defeated Ally in a doomed rearguard action, that in future British pilots (and French and Dutch and Belgian and Norwegian and Danish and Polish pilots who had managed to get away) would be operating from British airfields and in British skies. And he knew that he had a little time, perhaps almost enough, to repair some of the damage already done, to build up his squadrons for the assault which was coming as surely as tomorrow's dawn.

Behind Fighter Command stood Bomber and Coastal Commands, the Royal Navy, the Army however short of the mountain of equipment left behind perforce at Dunkirk, Lieutenant-General Sir Frederick Pile's Anti-Aircraft Command, the Royal Observer Corps, and the growing ranks of Civil Defence. But, as everyone knew, Fighter Command was the key.

Fighter Command was divided into four Groups. The most remote was Group Thirteen, Northern England and Scotland, based at Ponteland near Newcastle-upon-Tyne, under Air Vice-Marshal Richard Ernest Saul, DFC. The West had Group Ten, based at Box in Wiltshire, under Air Vice-Marshal Sir Christopher Joseph Quintin Brand, KBE, DSO, MC, DFC, a South African who when young had been a pioneer in long-distance flying and who knew all about night-fighting. For the South-East there were two Groups, Group Twelve based at Watnall in Nottinghamshire under Air Vice-Marshal Sir Trafford Leigh-Mallory, CB, DSO, and the all-important Group Eleven at Uxbridge under Air Vice-Marshal Sir Keith Rodney Park, MC, DFC, a quiet New Zealander of outstanding ability who had fought at Gallipoli and been wounded on the Somme, after which he had joined the Royal Flying Corps to become a fighter pilot. He was, as John Terraine says, the perfect conductor for Dowding's orchestra. It was an expanding orchestra now: by 7 July Groups Eleven, Twelve and Thirteen had nineteen Squadrons of Spitfires, twenty-five Squadrons of Hurricanes, six Squadrons of Blenheims and two Squadrons of Defiants, which on paper meant 644 aircraft but in reality were more like 500 available for operations, with theoretically over twelve hundred but actually 700 trained and experienced pilots. Along with these went the ground back-up, the Staffs of the various Command Headquarters, the Staffs of the Groups, Sectors and Stations, along with the Radar operators and the people responsible for storage, salvage and repair.

Both Churchill and Dowding saw the situation very simply. Churchill said that Hitler knew he must break us in this island or lose the war. Dowding knew that Germany must try to prepare the way for invasion, and that it was his business to prevent it. As it was certain that bombers would be sent against important war targets like ports and industrial centres as well as shipping, these had to be protected, which meant, as he had always foreseen, that it was no use hitting the enemy once he had dropped his bombs, he must be stopped before that. If Fighter Command were to win, as win it must, it would be by a narrow margin, far too narrow for anyone to gamble with, or to rely too much on chance and luck.

Solemnly he counted his assets. High among them came Radar. By now, Radar had developed sufficiently to make the vital difference in air defence. It might only be able to give just enough warning of approaching attacks, but just enough was enough for his purpose. Radar was not yet exact about the enemy's numbers, nor the height at which they were flying, but once they were sighted on the Radar screens the Observer Corps would go into action, and they were improving in skill and accuracy all the time. Radar operated through a fixed series of masts known as Chains, and by July there were fifty-one of these, twenty-one Chain Home and thirty Chain Home Low stations, whose rotating aerials could track the movements of aircraft and ships.

Then there was radio-monitoring. This had been a powerful asset in the previous war, enabling the Grand Fleet to set out three and a half hours ahead of the Kaiser's High Seas Fleet before the Battle of Jutland, giving the Royal Navy a vital advantage. Before the War was over, radio-monitoring had won the admiring comment that the movement of a single German picket-boat in harbour would be instantly reported to the Admiralty in London. As time went by and the Royal Air Force grew, its powers of radio interception grew also. It began serious close study of German signals in the autumn of 1939, and in February 1940 Flight Lieutenant (later Group Captain) Scott Farnie set up the first listening-post at Hawkinge, later transferred further inland for safety to Kingsdown. This marked the start of the invaluable 'Y Service', which kept a round-the-clock surveillance of German messages and was one of the War's best-kept secrets.

Those who have read Barbara W Tuchman's splendid book The Zimmermann Telegram will remember how enthralling it was to follow the processes of deciphering and decoding in the obscure suite of chambers opening off room 40 in the Admiralty Old Building. Room 40 OB was an address that provoked no interest, but it became a legend among cryptographers, and now, a generation later, Room 40 OB's spiritual descendants were working to capture every German signal out of the air and pass its knowledge on directly to Bentley Priory. 'Y Service' recruited English people, especially women, who were fluent in German, and they rapidly became so practised in interpreting what they heard that they could identify each type of German aircraft, which proved a blessing indeed. But at first they had no means of warning in time the Royal Air Force pilots already in the air that the Luftwaffe had spotted them, and could only sit helplessly at their instruments hearing warning shouts like Indianer unten fünf Uhr (bandits below at five o'clock) which they could not pass on to the 'bandits' themselves. With the passage of time, however, this difficulty was overcome and 'Y Service' was able to take less than a minute between hearing the signal and sending it on.

'Y Service' depended a good deal upon 'Station X' at Bletchley Park, the site of the Government Code and Cipher School, where brilliant operators broke the German codes. This service, beyond price as it was at once known to be, gave a powerful reinforcement to Dowding and his staffs with its fast transmission of precise information. All eavesdropping upon an enemy starts from the intercept, and, what with 'Station X', 'Y Service', and Radar, many lives and aircraft were saved which might otherwise have been thrown away in comparatively aimless patrols searching an empty sky.

Of course with the Luftwaffe established on French, Belgian and Dutch airfields most of their signals were sent by land-line, which was no use to 'Station X'. But fortunately the Luftwaffe operated its air signals so negligently that it was easy for Bletchley Park to interpret whatever it picked up. At first its messages came by way of the Air Ministry, but after a shorter interval than anyone had a right to expect they came direct by teleprinter and were passed straight on to Bentley Priory, to the Special Liaison Unit in a sound-proof room next door to the Operations Room itself.

An additional source of help came from the General Post Office, which, in the eighteen months between the Munich crisis and the end of the 'phoney war', had been building, very efficiently and in complete secrecy, a special network of emergency telephone lines, with a Defence Teleprinter network alongside.

The heart of Bentley Priory was the Operations Room, called by everyone the Ops Room, which in March 1940 had been put into a kind of concrete bunker in the basement. Next to it were not only the Special Liaison Unit but also a so-called filter centre where all information from the Radar Chains and from the Observer Corps was cross-checked before it was passed on to the Ops Room itself. Here the Women's Auxiliary Air Force girls moved the pieces on the huge table-map with their 'croupier' rakes, a scene familiar to all who saw some of the excellent contemporary films with Royal Air Force scenes in them. In the Ops Room aircraft tracks over the whole of Britain and the surrounding waters were shown, making it the only place from which Fighter Command could be controlled as a whole. Information flowed from it to the other Ops Rooms, where the maps showed Group areas and their immediate surroundings. From Group Ops Rooms the relevant gen (the Royal Air Force's own word for information) went to the Sector Ops Rooms. The Sectors dealt directly with the squadrons, for their job was to get squadrons into the air at the right place with every possible piece of relevant information, and then, when combats were over, guiding them safely back. The Sector Controllers' responsibilities therefore broke off in the middle, so to speak, lasting until their fighter pilots caught sight of the enemy, and beginning again as each action was ended and the aircraft turned for home. So their importance was crucial. They were usually officers of Squadron Leader or Wing Commander rank. The Official History says that they needed the keenest intuitive judgment, and their function was unique to the Royal Air Force, for it was not possible for Lieutenant-Commanders or Commanders in the Royal Navy or for Majors or Lieutenant-Colonels in the Army to play this rôle, dealing as those Services did with much larger numbers at a time. The Air Staff had originally suggested Signals Branch officers for the job, but it was soon seen that the pilots preferred 'one of themselves', meaning men with combat experience. To the pilots their voices came as friendly, unruffled, understanding and somehow familiar, bringing a sense of reassuring support to the young chevaliers in the air. The word 'young' is the key: very few of them were more than twenty-five, and they were incorrigibly light-hearted about all they did, not thinking of sounding solemn about the dangers they encountered or the glories they achieved. Many civilians, then and later, thought they looked far too young to have earned the medal-ribbons they wore, more of them as time went on. But earned them they certainly had.

Any country at war needs to find out every possible scrap of information about the enemy, in particular about his order of battle. This phrase means the master plan, the details in his documentary statements regarding all his fighting Services, the size of each unit, its equipment, and where it is at any given time. There has already been a mention of 'Station X': an additional word about this should be included.

In 1938, in a factory in East Germany, special machines were being made for sending signals in code. One of the mechanics was Polish, and he observed and noted with interest what the various machine-parts were, how they were put together, and how they were designed to function. Later, the Germans found out what his nationality was, gave him the sack and sent him back to Poland. In Warsaw he got in touch with the Polish Secret Service, and told them what he had seen, whereupon they made contact with the Secret Service people in London and Paris. The young man was carefully smuggled out of Poland with false papers and quietly brought to the French capital, where the Deuxième Bureau gave him a workshop and an assistant carpenter and asked him to make a wooden copy of the machine, the bigger the better to include as much detail as possible. The result looked rather like the open top half of an upright piano. Drawings of most code and cipher machines known to exist anywhere in the world could be found in most Secret Service files, and what the wooden copy showed enabled London to identify the machine the Germans called the Enigma. Co-operation between the Secret Services of Britain, France and Poland, together with the help of Poles working under German names in Germany, made it possible for a brand new complete Enigma machine to be stolen from its factory without anyone in authority knowing of the theft, and it was brought safely to England. It was installed at Bletchley Park, 'Station X', where the team of brilliant mathematical experts at decoding and deciphering went to work on it. They used the new and alarming science of electronics to work out what have in this context been charmingly called the Enigma Variations, and made a machine of their own to interpret them. From that moment on, when the first experimental Enigma messages were sent out in February 1940 and neatly caught and deciphered at Bletchley Park, the worst problems faced by the wizards there were the eternal ones faced by the successful decoder: how to make good use of information gained without revealing that the code had been broken. But it was done, and done in close collaboration with Bentley Priory. Just as the Radar people learnt how to bend the radio beams on which the Germans relied to lead them unerringly to their bombing-targets, so 'Ultra' (a shortened version of 'Ultra Secret') deciphered the code messages picked out of the air and let Dowding know where and when he could expect attacks, and in what strength. The Germans never found out.

Bletchley Park was the key place for this work in the summer and autumn of 1940, but 'Ultra' went on serving right through the War, supplying vital knowledge not only to Bomber Command and the rest of the Royal Air Force but to the Royal Navy and the Army. It functioned on battlefields that spanned oceans and entered other continents, notably in North Africa. And of course this was not Bletchley Park's sole function. For example, early in the War its officers had been responsible for obtaining clear and accurate air photographs of airfields in Europe: in April 1940, for instance, Spitfires painted pale eggshell blue and therefore virtually invisible flew at 30,000 feet to photograph every airfield in Belgium.

This whole structure of strategy, tactics, information, briefing and command interlocked as an admirable instrument of war. It was not suited to the occasional awkward or maverick character, but it was just right for the many who could benefit from instructions before and after action, while being able to improvise brilliantly in combat. In combat, brilliant improvisation was of the essence.

It was soon clear to Fighter Command that the experiences of the Battle of France had not fully sunk in with everybody. There were some squadrons still operating in the old V-formations of three aircraft, which could all too easily fall victim to German tactics. The German fighters flew in pairs, two machines about two hundred yards apart, which meant that they could concentrate on covering each other. Sometimes there were two pairs together. Fighter Command learnt to adopt the same style because it obviously brought better results. The Royal Air Force called it a 'four-finger' formation, as, using two pairs, they flew with the aircraft positioned like the fingertips of an outstretched hand. The great advantage of this formation was that the loose pairs or fours could guard against being 'jumped' and could give their full attention to the combat itself.

But the Germans had made discoveries too. Their first unpleasant surprise was the comparatively poor showing of the Messerschmidt 110. They had suspected it before, when the 110 had met Hurricanes over France and had been forced to circle defensively. Now over England the 110 was all too easy to dismiss when escorting bombers. This meant that more than two hundred German fighters were virtually useless, and the full responsibility passed to the Messerschmidt 109. Superb it was, but it had increasingly to outnumber the bombers it was guarding by as much as three to one, and the bomber crews liked their escort to fly close, which prevented the 109 from using its brilliant combat powers to the full. In addition, a reserve force of fighters had to be kept back to protect damaged German aircraft pursued by British fighters as they limped back towards the French coast. There was another snag too. The limitations of the 109 range shortened the distances the whole force could fly and the length of time it could spend over the target before turning back. The limit of the range was London, which is why the air battles of the period took place over south-eastern England, and therefore why it was fought, as he had always believed it must be, on Dowding's terms.

So it was Group Eleven that fought the preliminary battle in the second half of June and much of July, until Group Ten joined in. This put Group Eleven's Commander, Sir Keith Park, in a key position, with his Group at the centre of the fighting from first to last. His ideas, opinions and methods exactly suited Dowding's and he had the keenest awareness for every alteration in enemy tactics and for the smallest fluctuations and shifts of battle. Dowding had fought his lonely fight for his Command for years, so he deserves to stand alone, but Park was the man who in effect had said 'I will abide

Air Chief Marshal Lord Dowding talking with Battle of Britain pilots at North Weald Airfield, on the occasion of the Battle of Britain anniversary, 1945. Group Captain Douglas Bader is in the centre.

at thy left side and keep the bridge with thee' at precisely the right moment, so his name must be placed beneath Dowding's as, we might say, the architect's chief builder.

As anyone who knew him would expect, Dowding had reflected quietly on the likeliest ways the Germans would choose in getting, and establishing, a foothold on English soil. He knew what had happened in Norway, how by seizing a few airfields the Luftwaffe could pour in men and supplies very fast. He thought they would try to do the same in their assault on the south coast, with perhaps Hawkinge and Manston as the first airfields to capture. And once there the attack would spread, fought with little regard to the casualty-rate. It is always far harder to dislodge landed troops than to beat them off en route, so Fighter Command must make unremitting attacks on approaching aircraft whatever their type. Every fighter squadron within a hundred miles would be engaged. But at the same time the Royal Navy must be protected, for whether invasion came or not the war was lost if Great Britain lost command of the sea. When someone mentioned Stukas, Dowding engagingly remarked that they would be 'a conspicuous and attractive target'. He had an instinct for the points where strain would come and to take its measure in advance, like what to do when squadrons were reduced in numbers, how and from where to make the numbers up, and what to do if Ops Rooms suffered a direct hit.

Because speed and flexibility were so important, orders were always given in terms of squadrons. After all, from the moment of sighting the enemy the Squadron Commanders took over, as was only right. And it might be as well to mention here that, while a squadron in the air numbered twelve aircraft, on the ground it numbered sixteen. (This has been found confusing by a good many people.) By the beginning of July Dowding had forty-four squadrons, twenty-five of Hurricanes and nineteen of Spitfires, which meant 704 aircraft on the ground and 528 in the air. Divided as they were among the four Groups, and concentrating on the second figure (aircraft in the air), this meant that of the 528 which could be flying at any given time Group Eleven had 192, Group Ten 84, Group Twelve 132, and Group Thirteen 120.

This is why all planning was based on aircraft being ready for action rather than wandering speculatively about the sky looking for the enemy. The Germans did not grasp this. The vital thing was to get the fighters into the air at the right time, not too soon, not too late. This required the finest judgement, and on the whole that is what Fighter Command got. And because Fighter Command was there, and growing, and increasingly in the right place at the right time, the Royal Navy was not compelled to sacrifice major units in the Channel, and the Army, with so much of its equipment perforce lost at Dunkirk, did not have to face the Panzers. Not yet, any way.

After Dunkirk, both sides made regular patrols across the Channel. Some of these revisited particular areas, and the Luftwaffe pilots referred to the Dover–Ashford–Canterbury patrol as 'the milk run'. Maxwell recorded his surprised resentment at the Germans' trespassing, as he called it, in English air. German reports expressed admiration for each 'demonstration of courage by our old foe across the Channel', how hard he fought, how tough he was, yet invariably a clean fighter. A Luftwaffe pilot would refer to his single opponent as 'my Tommy' – an interesting echo of 1914–1918 terminology. As the summer went on, German failure to win air supremacy was 'entirely due to the determination and courage of the British fighter pilots' whose exploits 'will always remain a glorious chapter' in the history of war in the air. The disproportion often seen in the opposing numbers impressed the Germans, whereas to the British the sight of (say) forty Messerschmidt 109s and one Hurricane seemed so commonplace as to be hardly worth a comment: it looked perfectly natural.

A 109 shot up Maxwell on 8 June and he only just managed to get back to base, where the doctors found shell-splinter wounds in one leg and foot. He was flying again as soon as possible, of course. The comparatively elderly (twenty-six or so) and comparatively staid (compared with him) Sergeant Pilots thought him so brave, so ready to tackle anything German no matter what it was or in what numbers, as to be almost foolhardy.

Parrott makes some general comments of the greatest interest about the period from, roughly, mid-June to mid-July 1940. His squadron, between patrols, was making a number of training flights with new pilots who included two Poles and two volunteers from the Fleet Air Arm, vividly illustrating the current comparative shortage. (Maxwell mentioned this as well, saying that more than eighty experienced squadron and flight commanders had been lost.) One great consolation was Radar, which 'eliminated the need for standing patrols, and since the size of a raid could be identified, a section of aircraft could be scrambled to deal with a single aircraft. This gave considerable economy in flying hours compared with standing patrols.'

On Operations, a squadron went in four groups of three in two flights, Flight A which were Red and Yellow, Flight B which were Green and Blue, referred to individually as Red One, Red Two, Red Three, Yellow One and so on. (In contrast to the bombers which were designated by separate initials, A Apple, F Freddy, U Uncle for example.) Parrott continues:

The squadron intercepted some enemy reconnaissance aircraft and shot down some of these, usually over the Channel. Five Hurricanes were damaged by return fire from Heinkels and a Junkers 88 between the tenth and the thirty-first of July, but without any loss of pilots.

Squadrons took it in turn to be at one of three states of readiness, five minutes, fifteen minutes and thirty minutes. This last state gave people a chance to go back to the Mess for a bath, a meal and relaxation. For a few days at Tangmere one squadron at a time was completely released for twenty-four hours, midday to midday, but this did not last long and we were soon back to continuous readiness again. By this time we had more pilots and it was possible for individuals to be given a day off in turn.

Each squadron had four wooden huts on the South side of the airfield, the hangars, domestic sites and administrative buildings being on the north side. The pilots occupied one hut and the ground crew the other at each flight dispersal. The readiness aircraft, six from each flight, were dispersed on the airfield in front of the huts, with some distance between them to give some protection from possible strafing and bomb damage. Reserve aircraft and those being worked on were parked in sandbag blast shelters.

Most of the pilots at this time had seen quite a lot of action in France and over Dunkirk. All had had narrow escapes and most had had their aircraft damaged by the enemy at least once. Several had used their parachutes and others had made forced landings. And the strain was beginning to tell. Some were not sleeping well, others developed a nervous mannerism, and most of us jumped at the sound of a telephone bell which, in the flight hut, was usually followed by a shout of 'scramble'.

Those weeks were a period of waiting for Hitler's next move, which we expected to be aimed at invasion. Would we find ourselves strafing invasion barges in the Channel? Would we be without aircraft and forced into guerrilla warfare? Our Flight Commander, worried about the shortage of firearms after Dunkirk, looked around for a substitute. It so happened that we had plenty of Véry pistols as there was one for each aircraft, originally for firing recognition signals. There was also an abundant supply of cartridges. So, first of all, he removed the signal flare charge from a cartridge, leaving the propellant in situ, filled the vacant cavity with a miscellany of rusty nails and screws, and then replaced the cardboard cap in the end of the cartridge. He loaded the cartridge into the pistol which he then secured to the back of the flight hut, so that the pistol was pointing towards the ruined wall of a derelict farm building about forty feet away. Next he tied a string to the trigger and retreated some twenty feet behind the pistol.

I had been his reluctant assistant in the project so far, but none of the other half dozen pilots in the vicinity was aware of what was about to happen. He finally pulled the trigger string. There was an almighty bang, the gun broke from its moorings and sailed backwards, and there was a small cloud of dust where the shrapnel hit the wall. In front of the hut there was a chorus of expletives, plus a scream from somebody who had projected himself vertically out of his deck-chair and descended again when the chair, not surprisingly, collapsed round him. There was a unanimous vote that a Véry pistol would not be suitable for guerrilla warfare.

This, if somewhat outlandish, is one example of lessons learnt that summer. Others appear in reports. We have already noted the importance of fighter aircraft not flying in tight vics but more loosely: this lesson had now fully come home to the pilots, who had by now seen for themselves that a tight vic did not guard against the main danger, an enemy coming up fast behind. It was also clear by now that squadrons based near the south coast must not fly straight out to sea, they would not have time to reach the right height before they were engaged. Squadrons which assembled to discuss tactics did better than those which did not. It was essential to close within the correct firing-range, and all too easy to believe you were within it when in fact you were miles out. Errors of range-judgment were greatly reduced by the use of the camera-gun, for, whatever a pilot might think he was doing, the photographs, examined later, revealed details of aim and distance which were more convincing than any words. Another thing that only experience could teach was how short, how soon over, an action was – often just a matter of moments.

One point soon appreciated was that the trim uniform collars and ties were a great handicap to a man shot down into the sea. He was far too likely to be strangled. So the pilots adopted scarves instead, which became one of their trademarks.

One of these coastal actions took place when Flight Lieutenant Frank Howell led his Red Section up to 18,000 feet over Portland. It was an overcast day and they climbed through two layers of cloud. Howell caught sight of a Junkers 88 and attacked at once, shooting at it almost head-on. The Junkers at once jettisoned its four bombs and began to dive towards the water, just as Red Two and Red Three joined in. Howell had by then discovered that his port motor had ceased to turn and that some of the German bullets had pierced his radiator, for fumes were pouring out and the temperature-reading had, as he said later, gone right off the clock. He signalled that he was four miles off Poole and baling-out. As he floated down he saw three ships which, he knew, were bound to see him. He untied his shoe-laces, inflated his life-jacket, threw away his helmet while keeping the goggles, and then surveyed the scene. The tide was going out. He fell into the sea and stayed afloat until a twelve-foot motor-boat picked him up. The half-tumbler of whisky he was promptly given was a welcome gift indeed.

Miles away in a none too roomy field on a farm near Bristol, Flight Sergeant Michael Croskill was one of a group of airmen employed on night patrols which had been without incident for some time. Their first action was against a large force of bombers with fighter escort apparently heading for the Naval based near Portland. Croskill and his companions intercepted the attackers over the sea. Croskill, attacking from behind, shot down a Junkers 88 and saw its crew bale-out. He was then pursued by several Messerschmidt 109s, so, twisting nippily, he contrived to get behind the rear one and

RAF fighter pilots resting prior to take-off.

shoot him down. He now had the sky to himself as far as he could tell. But, back at the field, he found that the squadron had lost three aircraft in that action, and two experienced pilots had been killed.

Experience counted for much, but it was possible for a pilot without much of it to do well quickly. One Section that scrambled to intercept an enemy aircraft off the coast of East Anglia had two seasoned pilots, Flying Officer Haines and Flight Sergeant Steere, and one untried one, Flight Sergeant David Cox. He was the first to spot the Dornier 17, whereupon he called out 'Bandit!' and, as soon as he was within range, opened fire. Haines and Steere came in behind him. The Dornier caught fire and its crew baled-out. After this, said Cox, he was accepted as 'all right' by his squadron, and Haines took charge of him, having seen quite enough to feel confident that he would make a good pilot. Going into action with Haines did Cox a lot of good, he said, for he learnt a great deal which came in very useful in future exploits.

Pilots who found out how helpful searchlights could be were warm in praise of them. Squadron Leader Sandy Johnstone was based near Edinburgh where there was plenty going on, what with Glasgow and the Clyde one way and the east coast of Scotland the other. Johnstone's first shoot-down at night was successful because the searchlights caught the Heinkel with their cross-beams and gave Johnstone a perfect target. He was within a close range, too, for as his bullets hit the Heinkel's oil-tanks the oil sprayed out all over his windscreen, so for a moment he was flying blind. The searchlights, and Johnstone, followed the Heinkel down and saw it crash into the sea. Others saw it too: when Johnstone landed back on his airfield he found that his first burst of firing had been directly above it and the ground crew had seen the whole thing, which gave him much pleasure.

During the second half of July the Luftwaffe made bombing-raids on harbours and harbour installations. This was against the recommendations of the Wehrmacht, for harbours would be needed in an invasion and it would be best to leave them intact. But the Luftwaffe was itching to do some bombing somewhere, and they were forbidden to bomb the cities, as we have noted. The bombers were escorted by clouds of fighters, which provided the Royal Air Force with a two-pronged task: breaking up the formations to disperse or at any rate scatter the fighters, so that the bombers could be attacked before reaching their targets. It became customary for fighters to scramble in separate groups, one slightly later than the other, for this purpose.

The people of Great Britain were in a confident mood, seeing for themselves how well the Royal Air Force was doing. But the Germans were confident still, principally because of their greater numbers. They were getting ready to move into the really intense stages, the actual Battle of Britain itself. What this means is that they were ready in spirit. In strength it was perhaps a different matter. Was Goering not about to exclaim in pained astonishment: 'Is this my Luftwaffe?' Most commentators today consider that the period from the fall of France to the second week of August can be properly described as the curtain-raiser. The most sensible thing the Germans did, from their point of view, was to go for the English airfields, yet it remains true that, though such attacks left each one in a terrible mess, the worst hit of them was operational again within ten hours, thanks mainly to the devoted concentration of the ground crews. These had at the same time to keep repairs to the damaged Hurricanes and Spitfires going on at full speed: mending bullet-holes, freeing the jammed guns and making them ready to fire again, correcting faulty radio transmissions and oil-pressures. They made certain that, as far as was humanly possible, every squadron had its twelve operational aircraft and its four or six ready in reserve.

And we must not overlook the members of the Women's Auxiliary Air Force (known to one and all as WAAFS, pronounced by rhyme with gaffs) who were employed in Ops rooms as plotters. This does not mean conspirators. They arranged the plot of battle on the large table-top maps. In training they were taught to use the long plotting-rods with a magnet at one end and a battery at the other, with which the little metal arrows were picked up and correctly placed on the plotting-table according to the given grid reference. Those WAAFS who arrived in their Ops Rooms before May 1940 usually found themselves supplied with wooden sticks with a finger-stall pulled over one end as a grip, to push the arrows with, and the kind of croupier's rake to pull the arrows off, which tools were primitive in comparison. In practice the tables were so designed that it was possible to place the arrows by hand. The plotters wore headphones – the girls soon found that it was common sense to wipe these carefully before putting them on, to avoid throat-infections, an occupational hazard – and the grid references came through the headphones. Army officers were present to alert their anti-aircraft batteries when necessary.

Information reached each Sector from its Group HQ, and was received by 'Ops A', usually a woman, who entered the details on a pink form. She handed this to the Controller, who read it and passed it to his assistant, 'Ops B', who gave the order on his own telephone and then handed the form to 'Ops B-1', who ticked it as 'actioned' before passing it to the teleprinter operator for the records. Each plotter was connected to one of the appropriate Observer Corps posts.

Whereas each Sector's table map showed the Sector itself with its immediate surroundings, and that of each Group showed the Group area with its immediate surroundings, the one at Bentley Priory showed the whole of the United Kingdom marked in grids, and each plotter there had her headphones connected to a different Sector. Every air-raid had a number, and there were discs showing the estimated size of the raiding force. The small arrows were coloured to match the coloured sections of the wall time-clock, and had to be regularly adjusted to keep the battle-map in time with what was going on. The gallery at the back of the Bentley Priory Ops Room usually presented a mixed collection of people: Dowding himself, his Controllers, representative officers from balloon barrage, anti-aircraft, air raid warning and liaison staffs, and, of course, visiting dignitaries, who usually were considerate enough to pay their visits early in the morning.

Ops Rooms were lit by the new-fangled strip lighting, which the girls found rather a strain until they got used to it. Before May 1940 the atmosphere was relaxed and lively, with the evening shift coming on duty already dressed up for dates later in make-up, high heels and jewellery, and the girls brought their sewing and knitting for quiet periods. But as soon as the action in Western Europe got going all this had to change. From then on, the girls were in uniform and the needlework was left elsewhere. As things hotted up, some senior staff officers began to worry, for the girls could hear the airmen's words in combat, and some of the language was not fit for their ears. But the girls knew that men who are literally fighting for their lives are not subject to the same conventions as are men who are not, and they said firmly that they would not dream of asking to leave their jobs: though at the same time they appreciated the kindly thought behind the officers' concern.

The close ally of the Ops Rooms was the Radar Station, as a rule consisting of a few unimpressive-looking buildings, wooden huts more often than not, with the Radar equipment stowed safely, it was hoped, underground, except for the all too conspicuous Radar masts. The interior of the principal hut was a kind of miniature Ops Room, fitted with Radar screens on which approaching enemy forces appeared as 'blips'. Those studying the screens had to estimate the strength of these forces, learning to judge the blip that meant one solitary raider as distinct from the blip that meant fifty or a hundred. These estimates were received at Bentley Priory, which was important as, if reports of one Sector from its different stations showed a marked discrepancy on the part of one of them, this could be queried and re-checked. Airmen who before the War thought of a dozen aircraft as a lot now had to adjust to the notion of one raid embodying over three hundred attacking planes. Many an airman has said thankfully that, looking back on it now, Radar undoubtedly (in their words) saved our bacon. One of Radar's great functions was to put British aircraft of the right type into the right place at the right time, and one way of doing this that won much approval was to send up Spitfires to attack and, if possible, scatter the escorting enemy fighters, and then put the Hurricanes in to strike at the relatively defenceless bombers.

Some girls who had been enjoying a relatively carefree life in other WAAF jobs were disconcerted to be switched, on the grounds of intelligence, to plotting. One such had been loving her work in motor transport, driving her lorry all over the country, stopping at Army bases for petrol where she was invariably made much of and offered sherry and cigarettes. These transferred girls found plotting easy to learn in principle, but what was all-important was to develop the right speed while keeping perfectly accurate. And certainly none of them could doubt the crucial importance of what she was doing. The message sent in time to warn a pilot of an enemy closing on him could make the difference between life and death, and often did so. In this connexion it was vital for the officer speaking to a pilot to have a 'good voice' for the job – a reassuring, friendly and, above all, calm delivery. Voices are amplified by radio transmission, and the faintest tremor could give an unnerving impression of fright to an already strung-up combatant.

One thing that was certain was that the Defiants were being shot out of existence. The Boulton Paul Defiant, a two-seater fighter armed with four Browning machine-guns mounted in a turret behind the pilot, so that it could fire only from the rear, was too easy a prey for the Messerschmidts, and its rate of loss was horrifying – it was in fact withdrawn later, in August, for this reason. On 19 July, for example, nine Defiants of 14 Squadron took off from Hawkinge to patrol over Folkestone. They met a mixed force of Messerschmidts 109s and 110s, six of them were lost and a seventh was so badly damaged that its pilot only just managed to crash-land back at Hawkinge. One of the Messerschmidts did the same, jolting in low to crash-land at Saint-Inglevert in France. But only one.

Later the same day six Hurricanes of 43 Squadron left Tangmere with orders to patrol Selsey Bill at 10,000 feet. B Flight had led off and A Flight followed about 1,000 feet higher, both flying eastwards. Blue Two of B Flight gave the alarm of enemy aircraft in higher cloud flying the opposite way and, sure enough, a dozen Messerschmidt 109s appeared to A Flight. At once A Flight climbed through the clouds and then saw some more enemy aircraft, either 110s or Dorniers 17s, they had not enough time to be certain which, for the 109s had now seen them. The leader of A Flight, a Flight Lieutenant, gave the order to break formation and attack, and asked B Flight to go for the bombers. B Flight gave no sign of having heard. Just then a Control message told the Flight Lieutenant that these aircraft must be Spitfires – he was looking at the black crosses and swastikas, so he brusquely said so, and repeated the order to engage. He picked out one 109 moving in and out of the cloud layer, gave chase, shot him down and saw him crash into the sea some ten miles out from the coast between Selsey Bill and Bognor. He then climbed back up to 18,000 feet on his own and spotted three 109s ahead. He fired at the third one with all his remaining ammunition, and saw it falling, pouring black smoke and dropping bits. Seeing the other two heading for him, eight miles out and 16,000 feet up, he dived and twisted, hearing bullets hitting his armour-plating. His cockpit filled with smoke, his controls seized up, and a bullet struck his left ankle. There was nothing for it but to bale-out. As he floated down towards Worthing a 109 flew round him. The two pilots looked each other in the eye. The German pilot grinned, waved his hand and flew off. The Hurricane pilot, hugely relieved, took out and lit a cigarette. He then began to worry about smashing into the side of a house. In fact he brushed a roof and fell into a cucumber-frame in the garden, breaking his collar-bone and adding a cut to his left leg. A woman appeared with a cup of tea and a policeman leant over the wall holding out a glass of whisky. What with them, and the chivalrous German, the world suddenly seemed full of very nice people.

To many in the British Isles at the time the world seemed full of nice people. Churchill said that in May 1940 the nation found its soul, and indeed what had been earlier a collection of ill-assorted and often irresolute persons now presented an astonishingly vigorous and rejuvenated picture. Probably the classic example of this is the Home Guard. At first it was named the Local Defence Volunteers, a far less crisp and resounding title. It had been thought of amazingly early, all things considered, actually within days of the opening invasion in the West. A broadcast by the new Secretary of State for War, Anthony Eden, explained its purpose, in a speech on the BBC Home Service immediately after the nine o'clock news, the one programme everyone listened to. Mr Eden asked for British subjects, men between the ages of seventeen and sixty-five, to offer their services in an important part-time job – no volunteer need give up his own job to do it. He explained what it was, and said that all any man had to do was to hand in his name at the nearest police station. Before he finished speaking, the first men were on their way. Within twenty-four hours a quarter of a million had given their names. More than a million enrolled within a few weeks. Many were Great War veterans who longed for a military type of job. At first it was all makeshift: no uniforms, few weapons, premises for local units hard to find. Lords Lieutenants, as heads of their County Territorial Associations, did their best to provide former 'Terrier' drill-halls and offices. But premises were found or improvised somehow. The formulators of the plan had expected a retired colonel or major to take command of his local force, choosing his second-in-command who in turn would pick his junior officers and NCOs. But ex-colonels and ex-majors were not evenly distributed throughout the country. Towns like Bournemouth or Leamington Spa could form whole companies of senior officers, while inner cities would be hard put to it to find a couple of former sergeants. But the companies formed themselves as best they could. Whole office staffs volunteered. Government departments formed companies, like the Bacon and Ham or the Sugar and Starch divisions of the Ministry of Food. Members of Parliament formed a company and drilled in the courtyard of Westminster School. Golf clubs had few recruiting problems because members going on duty in fours could assemble early enough to play a round first.

There were pleasant incongruities: a former general who had commanded an army in 1918 had some trouble enrolling as a private, a former field marshal who also happened to be an earl became a sergeant in charge of communications. They all felt important, and they enjoyed themselves very much.

Apart from everyone's preoccupation with the prospect of enemy paratroops suddenly appearing (a subject which provided streams of cartoons in the newspapers and jokes on the wireless), the Home Guard's duties included making amateur road-blocks which, as the paratroops failed to arrive, soon became a confounded nuisance to all concerned (and would in fact have done very little to deter the sort of attack the Germans were capable of making), checking the identity cards which everyone was told to carry at all times, and clearing the way for strings of military lorries to pass from one camp or station to another. Home Guards on the çoast patrolled cliff paths, coastroads, and seaside fronts and promenades. It was doubtful at the time just how much the Home Guard could do to hamper, let alone halt, an invasion, and it looks impossible now, but that is not the point: the Home Guard was one example of an excellent feature of the summer of 1940, which was to make every individual feel valued, as if what he or she did really helped the war effort. Even the schoolchildren were not left out. Give as little trouble as possible, they were told, help others whenever you can, stick to your school-work and don't grumble: which is of course good advice to all children at all times.

As a pre-invasion preparation, place names were removed from the landscape. Station nameboards vanished, making way for station announcers whose voices, curiously enough, were far more clearly audible than they often are today. Road signposts were painted out, or removed altogether. Shops giving the local name now had that painted out, showing mysterious signs like The – Stores, or The – Tea-Shop. Of all restrictions, this vanishing of name signs was probably the most annoying. What to many people was the saddest was that the ringing of church bells was allowed only for the actual invasion alarm, so the bells could not be rung for anything else. It would be two and a half years before they were heard again, for the right reason this time (the victory at Alamein).

Many a busy doctor spoke scathingly about the Home Guard activities, as did the doctor in the enchanting film *Whisky Galore*. One country doctor in Kent was answering a call one night, driving his car near Hawkhurst, when he was stopped and asked to identify himself. This demand came from what the doctor saw as an uncouth youth carrying a monstrous ancient musket, which the doctor rather testily asked him to lay down before he did any damage with it. The young man did so while peering at the doctor's papers by the dim light of the car's side-lamps, which was all the illumination the law allowed. Finally the papers were handed back, the youth picked up his outlandish weapon and waved the doctor on.

Shortage of proper weapons was a great and understandable grievance to the Home Guard, who were for ever looking for substitutes. One rural company were offered a clutch of addled goose eggs to use instead of the hand grenades which they had not got. Knives on broomsticks were tried as pikes. Sporting guns were rich prizes.

Many a Royal Air Force lorry, or baled-out airman, or pilot who had to crash-land, encountered the Home Guard, and reacted with blessings or curses according to the circumstances. And occasionally the Home Guard had a real thrill, being the first on the scene to find a crash-landed or baled-out German. They deeply relished that.

95

And each day that passed without a sign of invasion was a day's experience, readiness and confidence gained.

6

Battle Order

Or what king, going to make war against another king, sitteth not down first, and consulteth whether he be able with ten thousand to meet him that cometh with twenty thousand?

The Gospel according to Saint Luke, XIV : 31

Fighter Command knew more or less what to expect. But only more or less. In war, this is always the case. What was certain was that they were kept busy, and that they were learning all the time.

One helpful lesson was the difference that searchlight batteries could make on night sorties. For instance, there was the night in June when Yellow Section of 66 Squadron took off from Coltishall to patrol the area between Wymondham and Bungay. The sky was perfectly clear and the moon shone brightly. The only problem for Pilot Officer Mather in Yellow One was that his radio transmission was so seriously affected by interference that it was useless. At half-past one in the morning of the 19th he was flying at 10,000 feet when he caught sight of a Heinkel 111 trapped in the cross-beams of four or five searchlights a few miles to the west, near Mildenhall. He climbed on his approach, for the Heinkel was about 5,000 feet higher than he was. By the time he came within a mile of it he realised that another fighter was already attacking, so he throttled back hard and waited for the other man to break off. He then closed in from behind. The Heinkel shot at him with what seemed like cannon, but failed to touch him, and as soon as he was within 200 yards' range he opened fire with two bursts of a couple of seconds each. The Heinkel made medium turns left and right. Mather watched it for half a minute but saw no sign that he had hit it. He had to report his action as inconclusive, though he did observe an aircraft on fire on the ground to the south. The most interesting part of his report is that it was the searchlights which enabled him to make the interception.

Dowding had stressed the need to go for the enemy bombers, which after all could do real damage. But the bombers came with fighter escorts, so there were plenty of opportunities for air battles of both kinds. At noon on Wednesday 10 July two German reconnaissance planes surveying a convoy near Ramsgate were driven off by the approach of British fighters, but they had time to report, and at one o'clock twenty Dornier 17 bombers and fifty escorting Messerschmidts were coming in. Six Hurricanes of 32 Squadron from Biggin Hill, who were covering the convoy, now off

An RAF fighter pilot goes aboard his plane in France, equipped with parachute and oxygen mask.

Dover, saw the German aircraft and engaged at once, while others flew to join them, to such effect that one of the leading Messerschmidt pilots reported that 'suddenly the sky was full of British fighters'. There were thirty Messerschmidt 110s, which were vulnerable from behind, where they had only one gun, so they formed into defensive circles to cover one another's tails, a practice that the Royal Air Force had observed before. There were twenty Messerschmidt 109s, but only sixteen got back. Three Hurricanes were lost. The main enemy force was unable to press home its attack.

85 (Hurricane) Squadron was then based at Martlesham, near Woodbridge in Suffolk. Its Flight Commander, Peter Townsend, we met when he warmly praised his Hurricane. On Thursday 11 July he was woken up and ordered to scramble: a Dornier 17 had been sighted off the Suffolk coast. It was a wet misty morning with poor visibility. The Dornier had dropped ten of its twenty bombs in Lowestoft harbour – the Luftwaffe was still forbidden to bomb ground targets by day – and had turned south when Townsend saw it. He was not yet close enough to fire, and was still not within range when the Dornier's rear-gunner opened fire on him. He replied, doing a good deal of damage to the Dornier's interior, sending fragments of metal crashing all over the place and wounding three of the four crew. The unharmed rear-gunner went on firing, and scored a hit at the exact moment when a shot from Townsend struck the gun from his grasp. The Dornier, bullet-ridden and damaged though it was, kept on flying, but Townsend's Hurricane began to drop down towards the sea, trailing black smoke. Townsend baled-out and was picked up by a small Hull trawler. He was made much of and dosed with rum, and was back on patrol that evening in another Hurricane. The Dornier crew, with makeshift bandages on, flew slowly homewards, trying in turn to jettison their ten remaining bombs, but these were wedged among entangled bits of wreckage and it was impossible to prod them loose. (No doubt, and luckily for them, the bombs had deflected some of Townsend's bullets.) The Dornier dragged back to its French airfield, where its crew found to their horror that the undercarriage would not retract and they had to squash gingerly down on the grass on top of the bombs. Fire-crews with an ambulance were waiting apprehensively. The crew got out all right, but there were 220 bullet-holes in the Dornier, some in the fuel-tanks and some in the engine. The Hull trawler was sunk two weeks later.

The eleventh of July was an eventful day. Six Spitfires of 54 Squadron from Manston spotted enemy aircraft, the sight of which faced their leader with a nasty problem. There was a Heinkel 59 rescue seaplane, not in camouflage paint but plain silver, with red crosses painted on it. It was escorted by twelve Messerschmidt 109s. With the lightning speed of thought, questions flashed through the Spitfire Flight Lieutenant's mind. If the Heinkel rescued a German pilot, wouldn't that pilot be back on Ops within hours? If it spotted British ships, wouldn't it at once report their position as a matter of course? Why, if it were just an innocent Red Cross plane, did it need that fighter escort? Didn't that mean it was expecting to be attacked? The answer to that was probably Yes, so the Flight Lieutenant ordered his Spitfires in. The Heinkel was shot down and lay floating on the water, one of the escorting 109s was shot down in flames and so was a Spitfire, and another 109 brushed right across the top of the Flight Lieutenant's own Spitfire, bending its propellers back almost flat, so that he had to crash-land in a field. But he soon had the answer to his questions. From that day on, all German rescue-planes were put into camouflage paint and equipped with guns.

At about noon that day Flight B of 87 Squadron was engaged over Portland against a force of Messerschmidt 110s. Among the pilots were Squadron Leader J S Dewar, DSO, DFC, and Flying Officer R L Clyde. Dewar shot down one Messerschmidt and then circled, partly to find out how the battle was going and partly to shake off two 110s behind him. He saw a bomb explode near a ship in the harbour and two 110s diving towards the coast. He had dodged one of his pursuers, but not the other, so he swung round behind it and it dived. Dewar followed, but his ammunition was low so he did not fire. At about 1,000 feet the 110 levelled out and made what were known as S-turns. Seeing this, Dewar closed and, at 100 yards' range, gave the 110 a three-second burst of fire. Vapour appeared from both engines of the 110 and Dewar had to throttle back sharply to avoid overshooting. The vapour petered out and the 110 flew on, with Dewar close behind. As no one shot at him, he stayed put, took careful aim and fired the rest of his ammunition, another three-second burst. The 110 flew in to land near Grange Heath. Dewar saw the two crew men in their yellow jackets climb out on to the grass: they were within yards of an Army unit so that was all right.

Meanwhile Clyde had an inconclusive duel with one of the Messerschmidts and then, seeing no enemy aircraft disengaged, joined another Hurricane attacking a Messerschmidt at about 6,000 feet. Both Hurricane pilots fired, the 110 went down to 3,000 feet and suddenly headed out to sea. Clyde's companion had run out of ammunition, so Clyde chased the 110 and fired at it. Vapour appeared and the 110 went still lower, Clyde followed and fired again. The Messerschmidt landed, a controlled landing Clyde called it, on the water near the lightship east of Portland Bill and near a smaller vessel which headed towards the 110, but it sank within half a minute and Clyde saw no one get out. The 110's rear-gunner had repeatedly fired at Clyde but had only scored a hit once, which split the central panel of the Hurricane's hood and struck the armour-plating near Clyde's head. He was at any rate able to report 'one conclusive'.

Two reports, two days apart, from 56 Squadron each contain one detail of the greatest interest.

On Saturday 13 July six Hurricanes were ordered to make a Channel sweep towards Calais, taking off from Rochford at a quarter to six in the afternoon of a fine clear day. They made the sweep without incident, but on the way home, about three miles off Calais, they saw about a dozen Junkers 87 flying at 7,000 feet with four escorting Heinkel 113s several thousand feet above them. The Hurricanes, flying in line astern, opened the attack, and the three in the leading Section each shot down one Junkers. Flight Lieutenant Coghlan confirmed seeing all three go into the sea, though, as Flying Officer Brooker and Flight Sergeant Cowsill had only seen their own targets crash, Coghlan's had to remain 'unconfirmed'. Following the first three, Squadron Leader Marton and Flight Sergeant Baker each claimed one, Baker seeing three splash-marks and one Junkers pancaking on the water. Flight Sergeants Smythe and Hillwood also thought they had scored, but it was not quite clear whether the Junkers they observed were their own or those previously seen by Coghlan. At this point the Heinkels attacked. Pilot Officer Page accounted for one of them, confirmed by Coghlan, who shot down another. Flight Sergeants Cowsill and Whitfield were shot down in their turn and were presumed lost, as a nearby destroyer searched for them without finding any trace.

Flight Sergeant Baker's Hurricane then developed engine trouble, but he managed to make a forced landing in a cornfield near Ditchling which did his aircraft some damage. He did not get back to North Weald until late on Tuesday, so his account could not be included in the preliminary report. The total scores for that action were listed as seven Junkers (two confirmed, five unconfirmed), two Heinkels (one confirmed), two Hurricanes and two pilots lost and one Hurricane damaged.

The subsequent report included the comment that when Baker got back he complained forcibly about his failure to get proper assistance at Ditchling airfield. This provided the item of interest: a pencilled note at the foot of the page, date 21 July, asking the Station Officer to obtain brief particulars from North Weald. It is signed 'K R Park'.

On Monday 15 July, in poor visibility with rain clouds low over the sea off Harwich, Blue Section of 56 Squadron were escorting a convoy at soon after two o'clock in the afternoon. Suddenly out of the clouds appeared Dornier 215 bombers diving to attack the convoy. They were in threes, in line astern or in echelon, so it was hard to determine how many there were: estimates show at least nine, probably twelve. Flight Lieutenant Gracie shot at one Dornier, which rolled over on to its back and went down, but he did not see it crash as he was being fired at with cannon, which he thought came from enemy fighters hidden in the cloud. Flight Sergeant Higginson fired at the Dorniers, all but two of which sheered off. One of the two scored a direct hit on one of the ships, which caught fire. Higginson fired at one of the Dorniers which dodged behind the other and did not reply, so he hoped he had put its gunner out of action. He attacked from behind and saw both Dorniers go down to sea level, one of them crashing into the sea. The report therefore gave claims of one Dornier 'probably' destroyed and one destroyed unconfirmed.

This report came from the Intelligence Officer at North Weald, who ended by noting that it was late as Higginson had gone on leave immediately after the action and it had to wait until he came back. This prompted another pencilled note from Air Vice-Marshal Park to the Station Officer, asking him to take this matter up with Beamish (Group Captain Victor Beamish), who, Park was sure, would not stand for this. Above the pencilled note, in ink, is the simple note: 'Done' with the date 31/7, and a squiggle of initials.

On that same 15 July 145 Squadron – Parrott's Squadron, it will be remembered – was in action. B Flight, Blue and Green Sections, took off on patrol shortly before seven in the evening. They were told to go above cloud, and found there were two layers of it, one reaching no higher than 2,000 feet and the other starting at 11,000. The space between the two layers was reasonably clear. Following orders, Blue Section went above the upper layer and Green Section stayed below it.

At about 7,000 feet the Green leader saw a Dornier 17 over 2,000 feet below him, ordered his Section into line astern and dived. The Dornier at once got back into the lower cloud. Green One and Three, wheeling left, followed it. Green Two overshot and flew south, which was lucky as it turned out because the Dornier emerged from the cloud ahead of him and he attacked instantly. He said later that this first burst took place a couple of miles south of Selsey Bill. There now followed a long chase, Green Two firing whenever he could see clearly enough and the Dornier making shallow

101

Two Dornier 17Z aircraft flying above fires started by bombs around Royal
Victoria Docks and Silvertown, West Ham, 7 September, 1940.

dives to evade him. The two aircraft were more than thirty miles out from the coast
of Sussex when Green Two ran out of ammunition, but by then the Dornier was down
to 100 feet, going more and more slowly, with its starboard engine on fire and flames
licking along the starboard wing. It was not, however, losing height, and its rear-
gunner was still firing, though none of his shots found a mark. With no ammunition
left, Green Two had to break off and go back to Tangmere, where he landed at ten
minutes past seven, and his report listed one Dornier 17 severely damaged.

The other two Green Hurricanes, having lost the Dornier in the cloud, were diverted
by a signal warning of a bandit flying west from Selsey. They saw a stick of bombs
fall near Wittering and then got a brief glimpse of another Dornier 17 above. Green
One fired quickly in the fleeting sighting he had before the cloud obscured the enemy
again. Green Three, pursuing, did the same, firing two bursts in two separate swift
glimpses. Both pilots, landing back at Tangmere at twenty to eight, reported that they
did not think they had scored a hit. The report ends with the laconic comment that
both Sections had taken off again since then to intercept more bandits.

On 19 July the Squadron's A Flight took off just after six in the morning and spotted their quarry, again a Dornier 17, flying at about 8,000 feet above cloud a couple of miles north-west of Redhill in Surrey. The Hurricanes were over the north-west suburbs of London and almost within range when the Dornier noticed them. It dived south into the cloud immediately and a long chase developed, Yellow section catching up with it on the northern outskirts of Brighton, where the cloud was much thinner. The Dornier went down to within a few feet of sea level and the Yellow section pilots could see many bullet-holes in its fuselage and tailplane. At this point Yellow One broke off in order to let the other two finish the job, while he watched what happened. He saw the shots find their target, flames coming out of its port engine and its progress becoming slower and slower, until at last its starboard wing went down and the aircraft crashed into the sea. This, he estimated, was some twenty miles south of Shoreham and the time was ten minutes to seven. As Yellow Two was the 'pipsqueak' (rearmost) aircraft it was the one that stayed circling the wreckage and calling up the rescue services. It returned to Tangmere at about half-past seven or just after, a quarter of an hour behind the other two. There were no Squadron casualties to report.

At the end of July, 145 Squadron was transferred to Tangmere's satellite airfield at Westhampnett near Goodwood, the first squadron to operate from there.

On 22 July, Flight B Blue Section of 46 Squadron was sent off at a quarter to five in the morning to patrol over a convoy thirty miles from Skegness. They found the convoy within half an hour, an easy sighting as it was firing its anti-aircraft guns. This showed the pilots where to look for the bandit, and, sure enough, there was a Dornier 17 flying west at 3,500 feet – the report says it was unmistakable in its normal camouflage and markings. It climbed to over 5,000 feet and, veering east, went into cloud. Blue Section followed and found it just half a mile ahead. The Blue leader ordered the attack, which was made from the port quarter, and the Dornier made a right-hand climbing turn and then dived straight down towards the sea, while fragments fell from its starboard engine and there was a flicker of flame and some black smoke. No more of this showed, however, through the subsequent bursts of firing from all three Hurricanes. The Dornier's top central gun fired at them but scored no hits, and its lower guns were silent. The most that could be written on the report was one unconfirmed. It looked doubtful, but the Dornier had quite a long way to go back to its base.

Two days later, Spitfires of 54 Squadron flew off from Rochford and saw eighteen Dorniers with a large escort of Messerschmidts approaching the Thames estuary. The Spitfires broke up the formation, shooting down one Dornier and firing at three Messerschmidt 109s. According to the Flight Leader, they all seemed to disappear from view within moments. The German pilots back at their base afterwards spoke of having a 'heavy scrap' and certainly shooting down a Spitfire but, they said, the opposition was 'formidable'. The convoy was unharmed. Early next morning another convoy sailed out of the Thames and turned south towards the Straits of Dover, escorted by two destroyers, HMS *Boreas* and HMS *Brilliant*. The convoy was attacked twice, first by nine German E-boats whose torpedoes sank two ships, then by Dornier and Junkers bombers which sank three more. The destroyers turned quickly towards the French coast and fired at coastal emplacements, but were severely mauled by the bombers and

103

Spitfire Mark II: Instrument panel.

had to struggle back to Dover. It certainly looked as though Fighter Command had more effect. There was another point too. The Germans had Radar (one of their Radar stations in France was Wagnerianly named Freya), but they used it to track shipping rather than aircraft, a mistake that was to prove costly. And all this time Bentley Priory was receiving hundreds of German messages which were sorted and translated with ever-increasing speed.

On 25 July Flight Lieutenant Powell led Red Section of 111 Squadron over Dover soon after three o' clock in the afternoon. There was a lot of anti-aircraft fire going on so he broke his Section off towards it, intercepting a Messerschmidt 109 which dived away from him. Just as he was about to open fire he realised that it was already being fired at by another aircraft, so he veered away, and found another 109 above him. It dived towards him, he pulled up and fired a three-second burst head-on. Bits of its central section fell off, one wheel broke loose, and as it flew overhead he saw that the central part showed a good deal of damage. According to his report, that enemy aircraft seemed more interested in pulling away than in concentrating on making a steady aim at him. He soon lost sight of it but at least he could claim one damaged. Powell's report ends with a comment that reflects an attractive hint of pique: he saw more enemy aircraft out over the Channel but before he could reach them they had scattered owing, he said, to repeated attacking approaches by Spitfires which he had to avoid by jinking.

There are scores of these combat reports, and many of them give an astonishing amount of detail. For example, there are two from 66 Squadron for 29 July. Blue Section, ordered at eight minutes past two in the afternoon to patrol Lowestoft at 15,000 feet, sighted a Heinkel 111 and, as was the custom, called out 'Tally Ho!' although, as the report put it, the actual order to intercept was not received for another two minutes. The Heinkel, flying north-north-west at an estimated speed of 160mph, stayed on course for a moment before turning south, whereupon Pilot Officer R W Oxspring in Blue One attacked from behind and then on the quarter and beam. Pilot Officer J R Studd in Blue Two attacked from in front and on the beam and saw tracer piercing the Heinkel's starboard engine and fuselage, after which he repeated his attack from the port side. Smoke poured from one engine after the other, pieces of the starboard engine fell off and then it caught fire. The Heinkel, which had not returned fire after the first burst, had by now come down to 8,000 feet, where it entered cloud 500 feet thick. As it emerged below this, the attack was renewed and it lowered its undercarriage as it came nearer the water.

Three other Hurricanes appeared and fired at the Heinkel from behind just before it touched the sea. Blue Three saw three of its crew climb out on to the fuselage and launch a dinghy, and the Hurricanes sprayed it with machine-gun fire.

Oxspring's Hurricanes had closed to fifty yards and he had fired 2,522 rounds in three-second bursts, with one stoppage caused by a cross-feed. Studd had closed to twenty yards and had fired 2,355 rounds in four bursts lasting altogether fifteen seconds, with two stoppages (misfire round, premature explosion). Pilot Officer J M Pickering in Blue Three had closed to thirty yards and had fired 2,800 rounds in four-second bursts with no stoppages, though he was caught in the slipstream in his first attack. His one complaint was that his windscreen had oiled up. None of the three pilots had been hit, and all their radio transmissions had worked well. They had taken off at ten minutes past two and landed back at thirty-five minutes past three.

Green Section made the second report. Ordered to patrol Hammond's Knoll at seven minutes to three in the afternoon, they were told at one minute past three to intercept another Heinkel 111. They gave the 'Tally Ho!' at a quarter past, on sighting the enemy about ten miles due east, flying at 9,000 feet. The Section formed line astern and turned in pursuit. The Heinkel turned slowly to port and the three Hurricanes delivered quarter and astern attacks, putting the Heinkel's port engine out of action, whereupon it began to lose height as it headed towards Yarmouth. About ten miles short of land it jettisoned six bombs. Every time the attackers came within 1,000 yards of it they noticed what they called a small amount of return fire, none of which was accurate. When the Heinkel was very near the coast it turned east-south-east and the last they saw of it was as it made its way eastwards, still losing height. The report states that it was very doubtful that it could reach the European coast.

Flight Lieutenant H F Burton in Green One had closed to less than 150 yards and had felt no slipstream effects. He fired 2,545 rounds in two- or three-second bursts, with one stoppage because of a misfire round. Flying Officer E W Campbell-Colquhoun in Green Two had closed to seventy-five yards and had likewise felt no slipstream effects. He fired 2,727 rounds with one stoppage because of a separated case. His aircraft was hit on the port wingtip but the damage was negligible. Both he and Burton spoke well of their radio transmission, and both said that they were using reflector-sights with plain glass, which in their opinion was not nearly so good as the green-tinted glass they had used on other occasions.

Pilot Officer L W Collingridge in Green Three, having fired 2,742 rounds with one stoppage for premature explosion, was called away for another interception before he could be questioned, but he had managed to complete his Pilot's Combat Report. Green Section had taken off at five minutes to three and landed back at a quarter to four, reporting enemy casualties as inconclusive. The place of attack was given as fourteen miles east of Hammond's Knoll.

Both reports were signed by the Squadron's Intelligence Officer, Pilot Officer J A Hutton. Neither report, unfortunately, names the airfield they came from, but the likeliest guess is Martlesham.

Some combat reports remark upon details of enemy camouflage paint, markings and insignia. The greater or lesser number of details given suggest greater or lesser pressure of events at the time.

It is worth noting that during this period 4 million tons of shipping passed through the Channel and 40,000 tons were sunk – one ton per thousand. Luftwaffe losses were 286, Fighter Command 148.

It is easy to overlook it, but there were other countries stirring in the summer of 1940. On 10 June Italy declared war on Britain and France. On the 17th, Russia began the full occupation of the Baltic states of Estonia, Latvia and Lithuania, an extension of her military occupation during the winter. On the 26th, she demanded from Romania the provinces of northern Bukovina and Bessarabia, and within a few days she got them.

Hitler was expecting the British to make terms. He had assumed that, once France had fallen, there would be nothing else for Britain to do. He hoped for it, as in that case a neutral British Isles would be no use to America as a base, and he would be safe enough in the West to turn his full strength against Russia. During the French armistice negotiations he said to General Jodl: 'The British have lost the War, but they don't yet know it. We must give them time, they will come round'. He had always got what he wanted by sitting back and waiting for an opponent's nerve to break, so he thought it would happen again. Also, he was not accustomed to thinking in terms of invasion across water. He was a Central European, a land animal, and an island mentality was quite foreign to his nature. So he waited.

On 20 June Goering had been appointed to the high-sounding post of Reichsmarschall – Marshal of State. Of course he saw this in terms of panoply, of ever more gorgeous uniforms and a richly decorated baton of office. He had, as we know, told Hitler that the Luftwaffe could break the British resistance on its own. Whether or not he knew of the Churchillian grand defiance and had brushed it aside as empty rhetoric we cannot be sure. But on 30 June he issued a personal Directive to his Luftwaffe, still at that stage the apple of his eye:

When re-grouped and in a full state of readiness the Luftwaffe will aim:

a) to create the conditions necessary for a successful campaign against the enemy's war industry and supply lines by defeating his air force, destroying its organisation on the ground, and disrupting his aircraft industry, thus defending Germany's own living space,

b) to dislocate Britain's supplies by attacking ports and harbour installations, ships bringing supplies into the country, and warships escorting them.

. . . So long as the enemy air force remains in being, the supreme principle of air warfare must be to attack it at every possible opportunity by day and by night, in the air and on the ground with priority over other tasks.

If he had made a careful analysis and review of the campaign up to then it would have been a sound move. But he did not do so, any more than he spent time thinking about new equipment and fresh training in the light of past experience.

There is some excuse for him, if not much. Thanks to the Messerschmidts, Junkers, Heinkels and Dorniers and the young men who flew them and the many more who serviced them and gave out the battle orders, and thanks to the Wehrmacht with its ten Panzer divisions, Hitler had become the master of Europe after two short campaigns, lasting altogether less than fifteen weeks. This, as A J P Taylor has said, was a triumph unequalled in European history. Napoleon had come nearest to such an achievement, but it had taken him ten years, and then it was not as complete. The victory in the West paid for itself and to spare: for example, in northern France and the Low Countries were airfields within comfortable range of England if they were going to be needed, and there was enough oil in France to fuel the Battle of Britain and the first assault on Russia. Occupation rates levied on the defeated countries could pay for an army 18 million strong. The whole thing had been accomplished at a remarkably low casualty figure in terms of modern war. Hitler was supreme from the

Messerschmidt Me 109E. 1,150hp Daimler DB.601A engine.

North Cape to the Pyrenees and from the French Atlantic coast to the frontier of Russia. South of the Pyrenees was Franco's neutral Spain, south of the Alps was Mussolini's Italy, now Hitler's ally. The two remaining neutral territories inside the spread of Hitler's conquests were Sweden and Switzerland, and these were tied into the European economic system, for Sweden had to export the iron ore that was essential to Germany, and Switzerland's precision instruments were equally important to the Germans. As he looked at the map of Europe, Hitler had every reason to glow with self-congratulation.

Except for one thing: that single recalcitrant group of islands in the North Sea.

It was plain that neither side was in any condition to mount either a full attack, or a full defence, immediately after the fall of France. Nevertheless, quite a number of people have said that if the Germans had sent a force – not necessarily a very big one, perhaps a brigade, provided it was a good one under a good commander – across the Channel at once, before England had time to recover her balance, they might well have pulled it off. But speculation of this kind is idle. The Germans were enjoying their victory. In Paris they were happy tourists, seeing all the incomparable sights, climbing Montmartre, going up the Eiffel Tower on which the swastika now flew, photographing everything, noticing cheerfully how many shops and restaurants now displayed signs reading *Ici on parle allemand*. The Luftwaffe, despite having heavy losses to make up, was flushed with success, with plenty of home leave in which to relax and enjoy being the conquering heroes, while Goering basked in their prestige and kept on announcing that his peerless squadrons could polish off the only enemy left with, so to speak, one hand tied behind them. He said he would require about four weeks, give or take a day or two, before the Luftwaffe was ready for the enterprise of England. And every day of that four weeks was a positive gain to the Royal Air Force.

Not all Goering's officers and men were so sanguine. After Dunkirk, as one Junkers pilot put it, 'Now we know what the enemy's mettle is like'. They had seen for themselves: their Chief had not.

If the Germans were to invade England, they must have a clear passage across the Channel. It sounds elementary put like that, but large enterprises start from elementary principles. The Royal Navy might be dispersed over wide seas and oceans, or be clustered in home waters, but, whichever it was, it existed, and it outnumbered the German Navy, except of course in the matter of submarines. In the Norwegian campaign Germany had lost ten of its twenty destroyers and three of its eight cruisers. Certainly it could not transport a vast invasion army, with all its arms, equipment and supplies, without having many more ships. And it must have a safe passage cleared for it. So the Luftwaffe would have to open the way to begin with, and before it could do that it must destroy the Royal Air Force and cripple the Royal Navy. It would be the first attempt in history to use air power to disable an enemy seriously enough for him to be unable to offer effective resistance. Properly carried out, air power alone might be enough to make the British ask for peace.

It is worth bearing in mind that Hitler never felt the same enthusiasm for attacks across water as for attacks across land. He did not join, let alone direct, the preliminary discussions for the projected invasion of England. For the only time in his career as a War Lord he left others to it, going off to his dearly-loved home at Berchtesgaden and not listening to anyone's opinions unless people came there to see him. One man with plenty of opinions was Grand Admiral Erich Raeder, a short, quiet man of considerable efficiency and the God-fearing attitude of many good sailors. Raeder knew how weakened the German Navy had been in the Norwegian campaign. The German Navy was in no way ready for battle. Raeder was thinking of a long-term plan, first to provide hundreds more U-boats to gain the mastery of the Atlantic and to stop supplies reaching England, which he thought should be achieved by the end of 1941, and second to create a full-scale High Seas Fleet, in the year after that. But only five per cent of German steel went to the Navy, and in 1940 there were fewer operational German submarines than in 1939.

The most extraordinary thing about proposals, discussions, or plans for the invasion of England was that for long stretches the Commanders were all in different places. Hitler was in Bavaria. Von Brauchitsch and Halder were at Fontainebleau. Raeder was in Berlin. And Goering was forty miles from Berlin at Karinhall, his private palace. The gulfs between the three Services were apparent. The Wehrmacht took the simple view that it would be someone else's business to put them across the Channel at the proper time, and in the right places, and then they would carry all before them. The Navy was full of doubts, about its own strength and about the supremacy of the Royal Navy.

So it really did look as thought it must be left to the Luftwaffe, which would be operating for the first time without regard to the forces of land and sea. Goering, never reluctant to make any pronouncement without thinking, or asking for details, remarked airily that four days' intensive bombing would wipe out the defences of southern England, the air defences in particular, and – say – four weeks of general air raids would destroy English communications and English morale as well, so that the way would lie open for what he described as a triumphant and bloodless crossing of the Channel. He gave no thought to how the Navy was going to manage that: somehow they would.

Hitler had no objection to his military Chiefs making a study of invasion possibilities. He might as well have some plans to look at. He thought, as he said on 2 July, that there was a chance, provided that Germany could gain and keep air supremacy and if 'certain other conditions' (he did not specify what these might be) could be fulfilled. The invasion plan, he added, had not yet 'taken any definite shape', so that what he was considering just then was 'only a possible operation'. Keitel had been heard to refer to the Royal Air Force as 'the last weapon which can be directly used against us'. He was right: for the next four years the only means of attacking Germany directly was to do it from the air.

When Hitler heard that on 3 July the British had attacked the French Fleet at Oran he did pause to think. The decision to order this was the most hateful of Churchill's life, but he felt compelled to take it, for anything was better than for the French warships to fall into German hands by default, and he dared not trust French promises. Who could tell what pressure the French might come under? This action could not be dismissed by Hitler as rhetoric, like a speech. It really began to look as though the British meant business. But how could they? They were in no position to fight. But if it were a bluff, then what a particularly savage one, to turn and rend an ally.

The High Command went on thinking and talking about invading England. First one then another put forward a comment, an idea, a theory, nothing yet that could be called a plan. Hitler, who was preparing an important speech for the Reichstag, still hoped that a peace settlement with England might be possible after all. During these weeks he seems to have been unusually vacillating, too likely to be influenced by the latest person to talk to him, not the assured and decisive leader he had been about the plans for the all-conquering campaign against France. He had ordered heavy artillery to be set up along the French coast opposite Dover, because those big guns would be needed to help cover a crossing, but there were many problems to be solved before that. On 11 July Raeder went to Berchtesgaden. Raeder stated the difficulties plainly. How could assault vehicles be safely landed? How could mines be laid to protect both flanks of the invasion force and yet not endanger that force while it was approaching the English coast? It would take quite a long time to make ready a fleet big enough to transport the great army required. Was it not far better to defeat the British by putting the British Isles in a state of siege? Submarines and bombers together could put a stranglehold on the islands. Invasion should be tried only when all else had failed: 'the last resort' he called it.

Hitler agreed, or seemed to agree, in a lukewarm way, with all this, but he still felt doubtful about the time it would take. He had his eye on the future, on the vast assault he wanted to make on Russia. That was the project closest to his heart. If only the British could be persuaded to make peace! Then his hands would be free, he could turn his back on the West and strike at the great enemy. What were the British waiting for? They had no chance of victory. Naturally he said nothing to Raeder about Russia, but he emphasised the last point. Why did Raeder seem to think that the English would not give way? They must be made to do so, by the means he had suggested.

This shifted the question back to the Luftwaffe. All their latest reports stressed the importance of destroying the Royal Air Force and the British armaments industry. The Luftwaffe's estimate was that it would take between two and four weeks to crush the Royal Air Force. On 12 July Jodl agreed that the Luftwaffe must pave the way: 'We can substitute command of the air for the naval supremacy we do not possess'. But he added a note of caution. Surprise was essential for a successful invasion, and surprise was out of the question so long as British planes were flying about and spotting what was going on. And the Royal Navy had still to be reckoned with. When Jodl told Raeder that, Raeder remembered that at Dunkirk the Luftwaffe had managed to sink only a quarter at most of the ships taking the troops off: nothing like good enough. What was more to the point, over the past three days the Luftwaffe had attacked three British convoys, sinking one small ship and shooting down thirteen British fighters, but they had lost twenty-three aircraft themselves. This did not look like an irresistible surge to victory. One distinguished officer said he had led 'squadrons of Messerschmidt 109s unmolested over British territory for half an hour at a time every day', which was obviously having an effect, for the British did not appear.

Other Luftwaffe pilots had reported this. At the outbreak of the western invasions the Luftwaffe strength had been just over four thousand machines: now, barely two months later, it was more like two and a half thousand. Their main activities were what Dr Karl Klee called fighter-sweeps, principally over water – the Channel and the southern part of the North Sea. They expected to attack whatever British aircraft or shipping they could find. As Fighter Command's priorities were to build up strength, guard the shipping, and go for enemy bombers, the Spitfires and Hurricanes were not always visible to the German fighter planes. The Luftwaffe interpreted this, not unnaturally at the time though with perhaps a shade of wishful thinking, as reluctance to give battle, which seemed to the Germans a kind of supremacy by default. Yet there was still no sign that Germany was going to be able to force a decision. Dr Klee called this period the Contact Phase, though it is not quite clear what type of contact he meant, nor how much of it there was. The officer who had spoken of flying unmolested said that the real enemy was the British fighter, so why not, he suggested, use the Messerschmidt 110s to escort the bombers and set the 109s free to go for every British fighter they saw? Like his superiors, he had never understood that it was deliberate tactics on Dowding's part for the Royal Air Force to concentrate on attacking the German bombers.

Now it was the Army's turn. On 13 July von Brauchitsch and Halder went to Berchtesgaden. They returned to draw up a plan, which turned out to look quite a big one. There should be three sections of coast to land on, Ramsgate–Bexhill,

Brighton–Hove, and Lyme Bay, taking off respectively from the Pas de Calais, Le Havre, and Cherbourg, starting with 90,000 men and within three days transporting 260,000. Before they could put this into a form fit to send to Hitler, however, a new Directive appeared, signed by Hitler on 16 July, which said in part:

> Since England, in spite of her hopeless military situation, shows no signs of being ready to come to an understanding, I have decided to prepare a landing operation against England, and, if necessary, to carry it out.
> The aim of this operation will be to eliminate the English homeland as a base for the prosecution of the war against Germany and, if necessary, to occupy it completely.
> Preparations for the entire operation must be completed by the middle of August.

The first of these preparations, he went on to say, must be that:

> the English Air Force must be so reduced morally and physically that it is unable to deliver any significant attack against the German crossing.

' . . . and, if *necessary, to carry it out*'. There is plenty of uncertainty here: all the problems he was already aware of lie behind that repeated phrase.

Raeder went quietly on listing the difficulties as he saw them. The invasion could be managed as long as no special problems arose and the Luftwaffe could get rid of the Royal Air Force, but it would bring the German economy to ruin. Transport would be so badly disrupted that the harvested crops would rot before they could be collected from the farms. If trawlers were going to be used for invasion transport they could not bring in fish. It would take the Navy ten days to carry the invasion force across. The Navy could not be sure of doing it this year, and very likely they could not do it at all unless they were confined to one narrow passage where the Channel was narrowest, the Straits of Dover. Von Brauchitsch and Halder were horrified. It looked as though the Navy would not be able to move for weeks, by which time the weather would be much worse. And only on that one narrow front too! Jodl then spoke to them, saying in strictest confidence, of which they must not breathe a word to a soul, that Hitler was immovably set on attacking Russia at the earliest moment, May 1941 probably. England could be smashed to pieces once Russia had been knocked out, which would be 'a matter of weeks'. Perhaps this was the answer? Halder wrote in his diary: 'If we cannot reach a decision against England, the danger remains'

Halder was sure it was better to defeat England first, right away. What might happen if she were left alone for nearly a year?

Hitler's Reichstag speech duly took place on 19 July. It included the following passage:

> In this hour I feel it to be my duty before my own conscience to appeal once more to reason and common sense in Great Britain as much as elsewhere. I consider myself in a position to make this appeal, since I am not a vanquished foe begging favours, but the victor, speaking in the name of reason. I can see no reason why this War need go on. I am grieved to think of the sacrifices it must claim.

The British press and broadcasting services both brushed this aside next day, and Parliament, deciding that it would make it seem too important if replied-to formally, did the same through a radio speech by the Foreign Secretary, Lord Halifax, on the 22nd. But the previous day Hitler had put the facts more bluntly than ever before. By now the invasion project had a name: Operation Sea Lion. Hitler said it was

> an exceptionally bold and daring undertaking. Even if the way is short, this is not just a river crossing, but the crossing of a sea which is dominated by the enemy. This is not a case of a single-crossing operation, as in Norway; operational surprise cannot be expected; a defensively prepared and utterly determined enemy faces us and dominates the sea area which we must use.

He warned in addition:

> For the Army operation forty divisions will be required. The most difficult part will be the material reinforcements and stores. We cannot count on supplies of any kind being available to us in England. . . . The time of year is an important factor, since the weather in the North Sea and in the Channel during the second half of September is very bad, and the fogs begin in the middle of October. The main operation therefore must be completed by September the fifteenth, for after that date co-operation between the Luftwaffe and the heavy weapons becomes too unreliable. But as air co-operation is decisive it must be regarded as the principal factor in fixing the date.

The Army General Staff were now keenly pushing ahead with their plans. Their Naval Adviser, however, was going about with a faintly pitying look, as much as to say: 'You don't know what you're up against'. Neither Army nor Navy had really noticed the significance of 'if necessary, to carry it out'. The note of doubt had escaped them. Von Brauchitsch, for instance, was brimming with confidence. 'It should be quite easy and should be all over in a month.'

On the last day of July Raeder, Keitel, Jodl, von Brauchitsch and Halder all met Hitler at Berchtesgaden. Hitler asked Raeder how the invasion preparations were going. Raeder replied that the invasion-barges and trawlers would be ready, the trawlers by 1 September, the barges by the 15th. Minesweeping was the Luftwaffe's job really, but full air cover was essential. Any landings should preferably be made a couple of hours after high tide, for an ebbing tide would securely ground the landing-craft on the beaches. As the Army wanted to land at dawn, they would need moonlight, which meant the third week in September. But still, on the whole, he thought it wiser to postpone Sea Lion until the following spring, May, perhaps.

Hitler said no. Preparations must go on for the time being (another note of doubt?). Everything would depend upon the air attack. He had ordered it to start as soon after 5 August as possible. By that he meant as soon as the Luftwaffe was ready, and when the weather was right. So the invasion must be prepared to start any time after 15 September. According to how the Luftwaffe was doing, he would decide whether to launch Sea Lion or to cancel it. Within a week or two it would be obvious whether the Luftwaffe were winning or not. This was the first time he had used the word *cancel*, and a quiver of surprise passed among the Army men present.

But what was Goering doing all this time? Nothing had been heard from him for several days, here they were at the end of July and the Luftwaffe ought to be ready. He sent Goering a curt message demanding that the Luftwaffe's attack-plans should be completed at once.

As a matter of fact, on that very same day Goering had called his Commanders to a meeting at The Hague. Each of them brought his Staff, so badges of rank and honour gleamed on all sides, with Goering as the focus-point in a dazzling white uniform encrusted with decorations. He told his eminent audience that Hitler had ordered him 'to crush Britain with my Luftwaffe'; There would be 'a series of very heavy blows' upon the enemy, 'whose morale is already at rock bottom', bringing him quickly to his knees. On no account must docks and harbour installations be destroyed, as they would be wanted for the invasion. Goering disliked talking about Sea Lion, because he did not believe it would work, so he spent little time on the subject, saying that the *Adlerangriff* (Eagles' Attack) was to go ahead and the Commanders were to let him have their plans as soon as they possibly could. In the south of Britain there were 'at most' four or five hundred fighters. The Luftwaffe would take thirteen days: five on attacks between ninety and sixty miles south of London, three days for attacks between sixty and thirty miles, the last five days inside a thirty-mile circle round London. That would do it. And for the first time a note of criticism sounded in his remarks. 'Those fighters of ours had better wake up. We're losing too many bombers and dive-bombers. The Messerschmidt 109s should be clearing the English fighters out of the way before our bombers arrive.'

There were murmurs, and one Commander looked so appalled that Goering noticed it. He asked what the man had to say. What he had to say was that during July, as he knew, there had been five to seven hundred British fighters in the London area alone, he had seen that for himself, and since then these numbers had increased, including many Spitfires. That, said Goering, was nonsense: 'Our information is excellent'. He added that the British were too cowardly to engage the German fighters. When the Commander pointed out that British Fighter Command had been ordered to avoid fighter duels, Goering said: 'That's the same thing'. How many Luftwaffe fighters would be used in the attack? 'All of them,' said Goering. And how many was that? Various figures were suggested. Apparently there were about 980 fighters and 1,100 bombers. But, said von Kesselring firmly, less than 700 bombers are ready for duty. Sperrle agreed.

Goering was stunned. 'Is this my Luftwaffe?'

Someone asked what figure the British Fighter Command would have to be reduced to in order to call it a defeat. 'Below three hundred.'

(Had they only known it, they were nearly there already. In south-east England Fighter Command had 312 operational fighters at that moment.)

One definite point emerged. Goering said, and repeated, that he had to have four or five days of good weather *guaranteed* before the all-out Eagles' Attack could begin. And, as it turned out, the weather refused to oblige.

Someone said something about bombing London. This was an idea that delighted

Goering, with pictures of Guernica, Warsaw and Rotterdam in his mind, but Hitler would not hear of it. The bombing of cities, which he called 'terror-attacks', were to be ordered by him personally, and by no one else, when the time was right, and he would know when the time was right.

The suggestion to bomb London had been put forward because it seemed the best way of forcing Fighter Command into battle. Very likely it sprang from the fact that the Messerschmidt 109, excellent though it was, had a limited range which, at its extreme limits, allowed for flight to the London area, twenty minutes' combat, and flight back. It might not be enough.

Goering issued an Order of the Day on 8 August. It could hardly be called precise.

From Reichsmarschall Goering to all units of Luftflotte Two, Three, and Five:
Operation *Adler*.
Within a short period you will wipe the British Air Force out of the sky. Heil Hitler.

Many German fighter pilots, before experience taught them to know better, imagined that the struggle over Britain would be a matter of fighter-duels, which they looked upon in an almost romantic light. The British fighter pilots knew that they had to go for the enemy bombers, which after all could do a great deal more damage.

We have seen a number of references in these pages to the inaccurate estimates of losses on both sides. Inaccuracies were inevitable. As so often happened, Dowding's attitude was cool and practical. When the Secretary of State for Air told him that he was troubled about the effect on America of the wide differences between the claims of the opposing sides, Dowding simply pointed out that the truth would soon be apparent. If the German figures were correct, then the Germans would be in London in a week. If their figures were not correct, they would not. David said that Fighter Command had been destroyed on paper three times over, so the Germans thought it was completely done in before Eagles' Day.

Neither side, for the most part, was consciously lying. For example, if a pilot, having fired at and hit an aircraft, saw it diving and pouring out smoke, he felt justified in claiming it, while another pilot from another squadron could come in to finish it off and claim it as well. When this happened in the Luftwaffe it helped to strengthen their belief that Fighter Command was as weak as they thought or hoped it was. One thing that misled Fighter Command on occasion was a habit the Luftwaffe developed to evade a sticky situation, flipping over on their backs and diving, which produced streams of smoke. Fighter Command had an agreeable practice when two pilots could claim a kill together: instead of saying 'half each' the senior pilot, with more kills to his credit, would tell the junior to claim it so that he could have a swastika, perhaps his first, painted on his aircraft. The over-claims, when they did come, usually came from pilots of different squadrons landing back at different bases. And, it is important to remember, there was often far too much going on in the few minutes of intense action to see everything clearly.

One point that it is as well to bear in mind, a point that is often overlooked, is that throughout most of 1940 Dowding was never quite sure whether, or when, he might

115

be retired. The date of his retirement was stated, and postponed, several times. This is a constant anxiety to anyone in such a situation, but to a man in Dowding's position, under the pressures of mortal combat, to have such a grave uncertainty always at the back of his mind was a burden the more grievous because it was quite unnecessary. This has been admitted, not without conscious shamefacedness, since. Yet all through 1940 he maintained his quiet, unwavering attitude, and was as punctilious as ever in thanking his Staff, whatever their rank, for good work done. Naturally his self-contained personality continued to annoy, puzzle or irritate those in high places who were less clear-sighted, less single-minded, or simply more romantic and emotionally expressive than he was. It is not given to every Commander to win a battle without any possible doubt, to know that he was the man who won it: and, after it was plain that he had done exactly that, when the Battle of Britain was over and won, those who had fought it said so in no uncertain terms. Johnstone, for instance, said that the great commanders, and the great battles, emerging later in the war would never have been heard of without appearing 'courtesy of Stuffy Dowding', and 'Ginger' Lacy, that splendid pilot, and he put the unanswerable question: 'Where would we have been if Stuffy had lost the battle?"

The confrontation between the Royal Air Force and the Luftwaffe during the summer and early autumn of 1940 was the only decisive battle in history, with a crucial effect upon all that happened subsequently, which was entirely an air battle. Taking that confrontation at its maximum possible length, from the fall of France to the end of October, it lasted 132 days, not quite nineteen weeks. But its effect was far greater than its length and scope. It provided the first proof, obvious enough to be understood all round the world, that the hitherto victorious forces of Hitler's Germany could be defeated. For the first time, those forces had to draw back without achieving their aim. This not only preserved these islands from invasion, but ensured that from now on Britain would provide a secure base for assaults against German-occupied Europe, culminating in the great liberating invasion which began on 6 June 1944.

So the whole period of this confrontation can be divided into phases or stages, and frequently has been, with hardly any two sets of divisions precisely alike. Before the middle of July came the complete withdrawal of all British forces from the Continent, along with all those Allied soldiers, sailors and airmen who could get away. The following month can be described as mainly exploratory on the part of the Germans, as they concentrated on the Channel and the southern and south-eastern coasts of England. The Royal Air Force meanwhile exercised its skills, built up its forces, and beat off enemy attacks, at the same time protecting shipping and coastal defences. The second half of August and the first week of September saw the Luftwaffe's strongest onslaught against Fighter Command itself, its airfields, aircraft and personnel. Had the Luftwaffe persisted with this kind of operation, the outcome might have been very different. But on 7 September the bombing of London began, leading to great air raids on other cities. By the end of October it was plain to the German High Command that any invasion of the British Isles had to be indefinitely postponed, if not abandoned altogether.

But – again it must be said – this was not clear at the time. Indeed, the term 'The

116

Battle of Britain' was not yet in common use. Battles are not normally given their names until they are over: for instance, Wellington named his battles after the place he had slept in the night before, therefore Waterloo rather than any of the other names on the map where the fighting took place. The Battle of Britain virtually named itself, going back to Churchill's remark in June that, with the Battle of France over, it was likely that the Battle of Britain was about to start. But the term was certainly not heard as a regular thing until much later, until, in fact, it was practically won. (The Germans, who date its start from 13 August, did not officially say it was over until the following March.)

Nelson had won his battles by superior freedom of manoeuvre and readiness in attack: what he wrote was curiously appropriate for Fighter Command in 1940. 'The moment they touch our coast, be it where it may, they are to be attacked by every man afloat and on shore. Never fear the event . . . No Captain can do very wrong if he places his Ship alongside that of an Enemy . . . and continue them there, without separating, until the business is decided'. This is what the Royal Air Force did in 1940, and it worked.

On 9 May the Royal Air Force was expecting battle sooner or later, though to the more eager it seemed to be unduly long in coming. Next day it abruptly arrived. As the only way to learn how to do a thing is to do it, Fighter Command learnt in combat, reconnaissance and patrol that they had excellent men and machines, intelligent and specific direction and guidance, and that they could therefore defeat a much larger, more experienced opponent, no matter how well equipped he was. That was the real achievement of May, June and July. Of course there was much confusion, many cruel losses especially among the Battle, Blenheim and Lysander squadrons (for example, in the Maastricht and Albert Canal attacks by seventy-one Battles and Blenheims, more than forty were lost), all the chaos of hurriedly pulling back from one beleaguered French airfield to another amid the tumult of war, and finally the untidy improvisations of getting out of Europe altogether. But by the time of Dunkirk a change was apparent. Fighter Command had, to use a cliché, learnt the hard way, but they had learnt all the same. And without the work they did and the men who died doing it in those first weeks the subsequent victory would not have been possible.

So now the framework of events, as it might be called, within which these exploits were performed stands out clearly. We can see it plainly today. The attack-plan put into effect by the Germans can hardly be faulted. Its results speak for themselves. Poland defeated in less than a month, Europe from the North Cape to the Pyrenees fallen under German mastery in just over two months. The execution was smooth and highly competent. The arguments, changes of opinion, misgivings behind and during the second campaign were fractious and troubled. But it worked in the most conclusive manner. And then, when all seemed clear, the War all but over, at any rate to the watching world, the next stage of the German plans was seamed and rent by dissension, when the seemingly straightforward central issues, the invasion and rapid conquest of the British Isles, suddenly bristled with difficulties. Every day that passed after 22 June was a priceless day gained for the British, a chance lost for the Germans. And in the end, of course, they had indeed left it too late.

Studies of past wars show how much always depended on the weather and the time of year. In the twentieth century, when wars went on throughout the year and round the clock, it might seem as if the weather no longer mattered. After all, it is well known that the armies of the past could not fight in winter, when the roads were impassable, nor at the time of the spring sowing, while everything had to stop while the harvest was got in. People may be forgiven for thinking that all that had changed, when they read of the Great War of 1914–1918 which, to judge by reports, records and files, went on without pause for four years and fourteen weeks. Yet there were many days in that War when all that the men on either side could do was to stay in their trenches firing shells from time to time, while a few miles behind both vast armies the annual experiences of ploughing and sowing, reaping and mowing, and trying to move on waterlogged or snowbound roads went on as inexorably as ever. And despite all the technical improvements that developed, the tank and the aeroplane were still hampered by storm and tempest, fog and ice, and no naval commander in his senses would contemplate putting an invasion fleet to sea without a prospect of reasonably calm weather. The War of 1939–1945 illustrates this perfectly. The phrase 'bombers' moon' was not used for nothing, the German tanks were frozen in their tracks in Russia and lay helpless, the invasion of occupied Europe was made in June. It was therefore not only natural but sensible for the German High Command to take it for granted that if Britain had not been invaded before October 1940 it could not be invaded before the spring of 1941. Few people in England had really worked this out in their minds at the time, and those who had kept very quiet about it, rather than slacken the country's resolute state of expectancy and readiness. Meanwhile, British confidence grew with every passing day. In a peculiar way the blitz helped, for a danger encountered is usually a good deal less alarming than a danger anticipated. (Incidentally, the word 'blitz' used in this context is one of many English examples of giving a foreign word a meaning very different from its native usage. 'Blitz' means 'lightning'. Whatever the air raids could be called, they were emphatically not lightning, but ground on for hours at a time.) We know now that Hitler postponed invasion 'until further notice' on 17 September and put it off 'indefinitely' on 12 October. The fact remains that he had been so sure, or had so convinced himself, that Britain would agree to a long truce, if not a peace settlement, once France had fallen, that he had not really thought carefully about invasion, as we know. What outward preparations the Germans made were improvised, hit or miss in character, scrambled together without any of the meticulous precision that had carried the Wehrmacht to victory in France. This is obvious from the British reconnaissance reports, pilots telling of barges clustered about ports and river-mouths across the Channel. Many, probably most, of these barges had been built for river and canal traffic, and were perfectly adequate and serviceable on such comparatively tranquil waters, but what would they do in a choppy stretch of open sea?

It is easy, too easy, to ask pertinent and difficult questions long after the event, when facts unknown or unrealised at the time have eventually come to light. One of these troublesome questions has been: as fighter aircraft were the key to success in battle in 1940, might it not after all have been better to throw the entire resources of Fighter Command into the Battle of France? Does any taint of guilt on this point still cling to Dowding? A force of fighters large enough could have checked the Stukas, prevented some at any rate of the bombing of French lines of communication the disruption of which left the French High Command helpless, and at worst would have given the French armies a better chance to halt the Panzer columns. But there is one conclusive point that dismisses this question as impractical, and it has nothing to do with Dowding. Extra squadrons could not have been accommodated, maintained and serviced on French airfields at that time, there was simply no room for them, and to do any good in the ways mentioned above they must have been based in France. The French not only had no room, they had no effective administration to provide any. And no one man, no one group of men, can be blamed for this – unless we go back twenty-one years, to 1919, the year of the Treaty of Versailles. The ink was hardly dry on that document when the *Entente Cordiale* between Britain and France began to lapse, and continued to dwindle away. Both countries had suffered enormous losses in the War just ended, both recoiled from it to lick their wounds and, if they could not forget, for they could never do that, they could try to push it back into the past where, they thought hopefully, it now belonged. They did not realise until far too late that the Great War had not really settled anything, that there would have to be a second instalment some day. Bismarck had said that a nation which has taken a beating will not rest until it has given one: and the beating of 1918 had not been unanswerably conclusive as that of 1945 was to be, nor did the men of 1919 yet understand that in wars involving millions the victors will emerge from it little better off than the vanquished.

There was another factor, too. The day that Dunkirk ended was, as it happens, the day on which Fighter Command was at its lowest point, lower than it was to be at any other time in the whole War. In six weeks the Royal Air Force had lost more than 900 aircraft, but, more importantly, they had lost 534 pilots – killed, missing or wounded – who would be far harder to replace than any machines. The Air Ministry's own historians have commented that Fighter Command in France could not have done more than they did, and they did it at a high cost indeed.

But now in July 1940 we mark the striking difference between the two opponents still on their feet. The Germans were rejoicing in their seemingly miraculous and rapid victory, their armed forces, especially the Luftwaffe, were thoroughly complacent. The British were not complacent at all, but they were exhilarated, free of complications, lively and expansive in mood, feeling oddly secure against all logic behind their moat, and, as has so often and so providentially been their custom, confident of coming through to the end. This was an instinctive, emotional feeling: they had never been particularly strong on logic. They did not feel defeated, therefore they had not been defeated. Certainly they expected to be bombed, but for everyone who seriously expected invasion there were nine – or nineteen or ninety-nine – who doubted very much whether it would come. It might be tried, but it would not get there. Philip of Spain had tried and failed, Napoleon had tried and failed. Both these men bestrode the narrow world like a colossus in their time, both had brought great and famous nations to defeat. But they had not conquered these islands. It was in the highest degree unlikely that Hitler could do better. There was the English Channel, that mighty deterrent, there was the Royal Navy which had never failed them yet, there was the Royal Air Force, that gallant young lot whose personnel they saw admiringly among them and on the cinema news reels. Truly indeed did Churchill express this in his history of the War, then he drew these same comparisons with these same would-be conquerors and came to the firm conclusion that 1940 outdid them all.

Every person old enough to remember that summer who has been spoken to concerning this book, whether military or civilian, has agreed that, mortally dangerous though it was, it was a curiously *happy* period. The people in these islands made it so, of course, but their vanguard was Fighter Command and the quiet man who commanded it.

The Germans received the order for the full attack on the Royal Air Force on 8 August 1940. General Henry Arnold, chief of the United States Army Air Force, said that, on that day, the British Fighter Command took off to save everything, and by the end of September they had done it. But it is worth remembering that they could not have done it without the men who had served in the Royal Air Force in the three months before that, who paved the way for them and made the victory possible.

Appendix

PRINCIPAL AIRCRAFT REFERRED TO IN THE TEXT: BRITISH

Bristol Blenheim

Mark IV: light bomber with three crew, all-metal stressed-skin construction. Engines: two 905hp Bristol Mercury XV. Armed: three 0.303 guns (one forward, one in dorsal turret, one in nose blister), bomb-load internal 1,000lbs, external 32lbs. Maximum speed 266mph, range 1,460 miles. Span 56ft, length 40ft, height 9ft 2½ins.

Fairey Battle

Neatly designed three-seat light bomber, all-metal stressed-skin construction. Engine: 1,030hp Rolls-Royce Merlin. Armed: one Browning forward, one Vickers-K aft, 1,000lb bomb load. Speed 210–214mph. Range 1,050 miles. Span 54ft, length 42ft 1¾ins, height 15ft 6ins.

Gloster Gladiator

Biplane, single-seat fighter, metal structure fabric-covered. Engine 840hp Bristol Mercury IX. Armed: four Browning guns. Speed 210–253mph. Span 32ft 3ins, length 27ft 5ins, height 10ft 4ins.

Hawker Hurricane

Single-seat fighter/fighter-bomber, metal structure with fabric cover fuselage. Engine: 1,030hp Rolls-Royce Merlin II or III. Speed 316–339mph. Armed: eight 0.303 guns. Span 40ft, length 31ft 5ins, height 13ft 1½ins.

Supermarine Spitfire

Mark I: single-seat fighter. Engine: 1,030hp Rolls-Royce Merlin II or III. Maximum speed 355mph. Armed: eight 0.303 guns. Span 36ft 10ins, length 24ft 11ins, height 12ft 0½in.

Westland Lysander

Two-seat Army Co-operative aircraft, metal structure with fabric cover fuselage. Engine: 1,890hp Bristol Mercury XII. Maximum operational speed 219mph. Armed: three 0.303 guns (two fixed forward, one manually operated in rear cockpit). Span 50ft, length 30ft 6ins, height 14ft 6ins.

PRINCIPAL AIRCRAFT MENTIONED IN THE TEXT: GERMAN

Dornier 17 Z-0

'The Flying Pencil', beautifully slim fuselage. Four-seat medium bomber. Engines: two BMW-Bramo 3238 Fafnir 9-cylinder radial air-cooled, 940–1,000hp. Armed: six MG 15 7.9mm guns (2 forward, 1 each side, 2 aft above and below fuselage). Speed 168–214mph, range 720 miles. Span 59ft $0^1/_3$in, length 51ft $9^1/_3$ins, height 14ft $11^1/_2$ins.

Heinkel 111

Five-seat medium bomber. Engines: two Daimler-Benz DB 601A-1 12-cylinder liquid-cooled, 1,015–1,100hp. Armed: five MG 15 7.9 guns (1 flexible front, 1 fixed nose, 1 each beam window, 1 flexible dorsal) and one MG 17in tail-cone. Speed 194–247mph, range 1,224–1,490 miles. Span 74ft $1^3/_4$ins, length 53ft $7^1/_2$ins, height 13ft $1^1/_2$ins.

Junkers 52

Medium bomber transport (with the Douglas DC-3 the most famous transport aircraft ever). Engines: three BMW 132A-3, 725hp at take-off. Armed: five MG 15 7.9 guns (1 dorsal, 1 in semi-retractable central 'dustbin', 1 aft dorsal, 1 each beam), also either ten 110-lb or two 551-lb bombs. Speed 130–172mph, range 620–810 miles. Span 95ft $11^1/_2$ins, length 62ft, height 18ft $2^1/_2$ins.

Junkers 87 B-1

Two-seat dive-bomber (Stuka). Engine: Junkers Jumo 210Ga 12-cylinder liquid-cooled, 600-640hp. Armed: two MG 17 guns (1 forward, 1 flexible rear cockpit) plus one 551-lb bomb. Speed 162–199mph. Span 45ft $3^1/_2$ins, length 35ft $5^1/_4$ins, height 12ft $9^1/_2$ins.

Junkers 88 A-1

Four-seat level and dive-bomber. Engines: two Junkers Jumo 211B-1 or G-1 12-cylinder liquid-cooled, 1,200-1,210hp. Armed: four MG 15 7.9 guns (1 fixed and 1 flexible forward, 2 flexible aft above and below), plus twenty-eight 110-lb and four 220-lb bombs maximum. Span 60ft $3^1/_4$ins, length 47ft $1^1/_3$ins, height 17ft $5^3/_4$ins.

Messerschmidt Bf 109E-1

Inspired design single-seat fighter. Engine: one Daimler-Benz DB 601A 12-cylinder liquid-cooled inverted-V, 1,050–1,175hp. Armed: two MG FF cannon in wings, two MG 17 guns in fuselage, one engine-mounted MG FF/M cannon with 200 rounds. Speed 205–340mph, range 410 miles. Span 32ft $4^1/_2$insins, length 28ft $4^1/_4$ins, height 8ft $2^1/_3$ins.

Messerschmidt 110 B-1

The Zerstörer (Destroyer), two- or three-seat long-range fighter. Engines: two Junkers Jumo 210Ga 12-cylinder liquid-cooled, 675–730hp. Armed: two 20-mm MG FF cannon, four MG 17 guns, one MG 15 7.9 flexible. Speed 198–283mph, range 1,070 miles. Span 55ft 5^1/3ins, length 41ft 4ins, height 11ft 4^2/3ins.

Bibliography

Of the many books consulted, the following proved particularly helpful. The first two are in a class by themselves.

The Right of the Line: The Royal Air Force in the European War of 1939–1945, by John Terraine (Hodder and Stoughton 1985)

To Lose A Battle, by Alistair Horne (Macmillan 1969)

Dowding and The Battle of Britain, by Robert Wright (Macdonald 1968)

Duel of Eagles, by Peter Townsend (Weidenfeld and Nicholson 1970)

Dunkirk: The British Evacuation 1940, by Robert Jackson (Arthur Barker 1976)

English History 1914–1945, by A. J. P. Taylor (Oxford 1965)

The Second World War, by A. J. P. Taylor (Penguin 1975)

Europe At War: A History in Sixty Cartoons, by David Low (Penguin 1941)

Fighter Squadron: A Memoir, by Wing Commander H. R. 'Dizzy' Allen (William Kimber 1979)

Hitler's War Directives, edited by H. R. Trevor-Roper (Pan 1966)

Middle East 1940–1944: A Study in Air Power, by Philip Guedalla (Hodder and Stoughton 1944)

The Narrow Margin, by Derek Wood and Derek Dempster (Arrow Books 1969)

The Royal Air Force 1939–1945, by Denis Richards and Hilary St George Saunders, (HMSO 1974)

Scramble: A Narrative History of the Battle of Britain, by Norman Gelb (Michael Joseph 1986)

The Strategic Air Offensive against Germany 1939–1945, by Sir Charles Webster and Noble Frankland (HMSO 1961)

Their Finest Hour, Volume Two of The Second World War, by Winston S. Churchill (Cassell 1951)

The Ultra Secret, by F. W. Winterbotham, CBE (Weidenfeld and Nicholson 1974)

Air War Over Europe 1939–1945, by C. Bowyer (William Kimber 1981)

Index

Military History Titles from The Crowood Press

From Vimy Ridge to the Rhine   Christopher Stone
Honour Satisfied   F Warren (Edited by Antony Bird)
It Never Snows in September   Robert J. Kershaw
The Last Battle   Charles Whiting
My Bit   George Ashurst
Papa Goes to War   Charles Whiting
Rally Once Again   Paddy Griffith
Unversed in Arms   P. D. Ravenscroft (Edited by Antony Bird)
A Sergeant Major's War   Ernest Shephard

For further information about these or other Crowood Press
 titles write to: The Crowood Press
                   Gipsy Lane
                   Swindon SN2 6DQ